COLLINS POC

BUYING YOUR HOME

Susan Heal

HarperCollins*Publishers*

HarperCollins Publishers
PO Box, Glasgow G4 0NB

First published 1997

Reprint 10 9 8 7 6 5 4 3 2 1 0

© Susan Heal 1997

ISBN 0 00 472053 9

Printed and bound in Great Britain by
Caledonian International Book Manufacturing Ltd, Glasgow G64

CONTENTS

CONTENTS

CONTENTS

Thanks to the following people and organisations for their invaluable help.

David Roach
Mark Gibbins
Michael Duke
Somerset Fire Brigade
Avon & Somerset Constabulary
Citizens Advice Bureau
NatWest

PART ONE
BUYING YOUR HOME

1. FINDING THE RIGHT PROPERTY

Deciding what you want

Buying a property is unlike any other purchase. You cannot exchange it or take it back for a refund, so it is vital that you decide *before* starting looking for the perfect home exactly what you want and need. If you are buying jointly with a friend or partner, or if you are moving as a family, you will need to sit down together and discuss what everyone expects from the new home. To do this it helps to jot down a list of things which are vital and a list of things which are preferable. Then all you have to do, when viewing properties which meet your vital requirements, is decide which one has that little something extra which appeals to you. For example:

Vital needs	*Preferable*
Price under £65,000	Downstairs cloakroom
3 bedrooms or more	Patio area in garden
On bus route into town	Separate dining room
Off-street parking	Garage

You may be tempted to compromise on one of your vital points if a particular property bowls you over, but always keep in mind what you really *need* from a property. Aesthetic qualities are all very well, but practical requirements are ultimately more important for your long term happiness. No matter how wonderful the kitchen is, or how beautifully tended the garden, these relatively minor aspects will soon loose their appeal if the property is in the wrong area, too small or more expensive than you can comfortably afford. Buy with your head and not your heart, and consider the lifespan of anything you feel tempted to pay extra for, like extravagant decoration, because high repayments will continue to be a financial burden long after the paint has faded.

- Don't lose sight of your priorities.
- Don't borrow what you cannot comfortably afford to repay.

- Don't buy what you cannot afford to repair and maintain.
- Don't be tempted by aesthetics which will fade.
- Always visit a property you like at least twice, preferably at different times of the day and on different days of the week.
- Don't be rushed into a decision by the estate agent or the current owner (often referred to as the *vendor*, but we shall use the term *seller*) who gives the impression that you will miss out if you do not buy quickly.
- Don't be persuaded that a property could fit your requirements if you do this or that. If you need a garage make sure you get one; don't accept the seller's assurance that the area on the side of a property could be put to this use unless there is planning permission and, more importantly, the price allows for construction.
- Satisfy yourself that you have seen all suitable properties for sale at that time. Don't just buy the first one which fits your minimum criteria.
- Don't view a property as an island. Remember that the surrounding area and adjacent properties affect the overall environment, especially where flats are concerned because the common parts (hallway, gardens etc.) directly reflect on all the flats in the block.
- Compare prices carefully and be thorough when looking at exactly what you get for your money in comparison with other similar properties.
- View properties in daylight, but do not be influenced by sunshine which gives an impression which is rosier than reality.
- Consider whether you could sell it if you needed to.

Choosing wisely

Buying a home is for most of us the single most important purchase we ever make. It is also the largest and most expensive, and yet many people enter into the process of finding the right property completely unprepared and ill-informed. It is not surprising then that so many buyers find themselves disappointed with their purchase because it does not fit their requirements. What is surprising is that first time buyers are not the only ones who fall into purchase traps; it is often the more experienced buyers who, complacent that they have 'done it all before', become blasé and then make mistakes.

• The gullible buyer

Gullible buyers are those who naïvely believe everything they read or are told about a property, regardless of the obvious fact that such information is supplied by those who hope to sell it (the current owner and selling agents), and may understandably be somewhat biased. Thankfully, and not before time, the Property Misdescription Act which came into effect in 1992 has gone some way towards stamping out the kind of elaborate and largely inaccurate property descriptions which used to be commonplace. Under the Act, estate agents, developers, builders and solicitors who sell property are all responsible for the accuracy of the information they give to potential buyers. Nevertheless, buyers still need to interpret correctly the information they receive, be satisfied that they know exactly what they are buying, and not deceive *themselves* by turning a blind eye to some disagreeable aspect of a property.

• The trusting buyer

Other buyers doomed to make a poor decision are those who labour under the belief that, should anything go wrong with their purchase, there are rules to protect them. Not true. A trusting buyer imagines that consumer laws extend to property purchases, so he makes little effort to protect himself. Whilst regulations exist to protect retail consumers, these regulations do not extend to property buyers, so there is no one to turn to if a property turns out to be 'faulty'. If you buy a bucket which does not hold water, it is clearly unfit for the purpose for which it was sold, and you have grounds for asking for a refund or replacement, but buy a property with a leaking roof and you are not protected by the same kind of statutory rights. In theory a buyer can sue a negligent surveyor or solicitor, but the procedure for such action is lengthy, complicated, expensive and carries no guarantee of success. So as far as property purchase is concerned, responsibility for ensuring the 'product' is suitable rests with the buyer.

- **The lazy buyer**

The buyer who cannot be bothered to put much effort into finding the right property will simply get what he deserves. He is likely to buy the wrong type of property for his needs, and stands very little chance of securing a good investment. There is no substitute for diligence when searching for the right property.

- **The 'bankrupt' buyer**

Those buyers who are unrealistic when calculating what they can afford, or else plunge themselves into debt because of temptation, are destined for financial ruin. Faced with the wide spectrum of property for sale, potentially bankrupt buyers naturally show a preference for the most appealing, and consequently higher priced, properties. Rather than accepting their financial limitations, they persuade themselves that they will be content to do without a car, holiday, and other luxuries, in order to afford the repayments. The end result is at best misery, at worst repossession.

- **The gambler**

The gambler assumes that the value of the property he buys will rise. This attitude carries a big risk, and a safer bet would be to have a flutter at the races. If you know what you are doing, it is possible to make money by renovating a property and then selling it at a profit. However, a general rise in property prices will only make you richer in real terms if you release the increased equity (the amount you could sell for, less what you bought for) by selling and then buying somewhere cheaper. Do not over-look the fact that property values can fall, which could leave you owing more on a mortgage than the property is worth (see *Negative equity*, Ch. 2).

Will it sell?

When choosing a property to buy, one of the biggest considerations to take on board, and one which is often ignored, is whether or not it will be easy to sell. If the current owners have been struggling to find a buyer for many months or even years, think about this or risk finding yourself in the same sorry position at some time in the future.

The exception would be a property which has not attracted a buyer because it is in poor condition. Provided the price reflects the present state and the condition is the *only* reason it has been slow to sell, and if you intend improving the property, the problem should then be resolved.

TAKE A TIP

If you buy a property which has been on the market for some time, you might find it difficult to sell in the future. Don't expect the agent or seller to be totally honest when asked how long a property has been on the market. Look at the photograph used on sales details for a clue. If you receive the details in summer but the photograph shows a winter scene, it has probably been on the market for many months – ask yourself why.

It is difficult to say exactly what makes a property easy to sell. It is considerably easier to sum up what might not. Location is all important. Someone once said that the three most important aspects of retail success are location, location and location, and the same rule applies more or less to properties. Those which are situated next to anything unsightly, like a petrol station or car park, and those near anything which attracts noise or disturbance, like a pub or chip shop, come high on the list of unsavoury locations. Busy roads, flight paths and rubbish tips are all generally worth avoiding. You may be content to put up with something unpopular, but will anyone else when you come to sell?

If your lender is reluctant to fund a particular purchase, take the hint – you may have trouble selling it later because any future buyers could experience the same funding problems.

What type of building?

When deciding on what type of property you want to buy, you might like to consider the pros and cons of different types of building. If your priorities are peace and quiet, and you are willing to pay the price, a detached house might be right for you. Semi-detached and terraced homes are generally cheaper than detached, but have the disadvantage of attached neighbours and the accompanying noise this can bring. You may consider, however, that close neighbours are both a security and a social advantage. Flats rarely have gardens, but this could be an advantage for those who do not have the time or energy to enjoy them. The lease may contain strict restrictions on what you can do with and in the property, and whilst external repair and maintenance of the building are not usually the direct responsibility of the leaseholder, maintenance costs and service charges could be high.

How much to spend?

In the property boom of the 1980s, many home buyers were keen to borrow as much as they possibly could, either because they anticipated their investment increasing (the bigger the investment the bigger the potential increase), or because property was so expensive that borrowing a large proportion of the purchase price was the only way many people could fund a purchase at all. The question then was not 'How much can I afford to borrow'? but rather 'What is the maximum I can borrow?'. To some extent this attitude has remained and many buyers automatically look to the higher end of their borrowing capacity – a trend sometimes encouraged by those whose livelihood relies on property sales and funding.

Deciding how much to spend on a property is not only a matter of how much you can raise for the purchase. It also depends on:

- The monthly mortgage repayments – how much you can comfortably afford to repay.
- How much debt you feel confident to carry. If you have reason to worry about job security, this may affect your decision on how much to borrow or whether to buy at all.
- Your future needs. If you intend extending your family, for instance, it might be more cost effective to buy a larger property in the first place, rather than incurring a second set of sale and purchase costs later.

- Whether you see your home as a status symbol or simply somewhere to live. You do not *have* to buy the biggest and most impressive home you can afford. If a cheaper property meets your needs, why pay more?
- How much equity or savings you have. The financial demands involved in a purchase (surveyors fees, conveyance costs etc.), on top of the purchase cost itself, may eat away at the savings you intended putting towards the purchase price. This will necessitate either borrowing more than originally envisaged or else buying a slightly cheaper property.

Decide how much you want (and can afford) to spend by speaking to your chosen lender. Arrange provisional funding, then look at property up to that amount. That way you start your hunt knowing your upper limit, instead of wasting time looking at properties you cannot realistically afford.

Using estate agents

For most prospective buyers, the first step is to visit estate agents in the vicinity to find out what properties are currently for sale. However, do not rely on estate agents to understand fully what you want, need or can afford, or to give complete information about areas, individual properties, or the position, financial or otherwise, of the current owners. Neither should estate agents be the only source of financial advice.

Estate agents are an invaluable market-place for sellers to display their wares and for buyers to see what is available; no one could deny that, and most of them are prepared to work very hard to match the right buyer with the right property. However, their business is not a vocation to ensure the comfort and satisfaction of the nation, so keep to the forefront of your mind that estate agents are purely there to sell property – to whom is of little concern. To an agent a satisfied buyer is not nearly as important as a satisfied seller – it is the seller who pays the agent's fee.

Registering with agents

Registering with an agent is a simple process. Either telephone or call in to the agent's office and ask to be put on the mailing list. The agent will make a note of your name and contact address together with details of the type of property you are looking for, such as the number of bedrooms needed, preferred location and maximum price, and will then send you written details of any properties which fit these requirements. You may be asked questions about your own sale, if applicable, and what funding arrangements you have made. This is not to satisfy the agent's curiosity, but because the information given may influence whether or not an applicant's subsequent offer is accepted (see *Buying Positions*, below). If you are not in a position to proceed with a purchase quickly, perhaps because you have to sell your current property first, or because provisional funding has not been arranged, the agent is unlikely to recommend your offer to his client (the seller).

If you call into an agency to register in person, you will usually be given a batch of property details there and then. There is no charge for registering with an estate agent, and you (the applicant) are under no obligation to buy or view any property. If and when you receive details of a property you like the look of and which warrants closer inspection, contact the agency who will make an appointment for you to view it. The agent may or may not accompany you during a viewing, depending on whether this has been requested by the seller. If the property is empty or the appointment is inconvenient for the seller, the agent will meet you there with a key.

Your may receive details of the same property from several different agents, and if this happens it matters not which agency you approach to arrange a viewing. Receiving the same details from several agents may give the impression that the current owners are having difficulty finding a buyer, but this is not always the case, and it could be that they are keen to sell quickly by reaching as many potential buyers as possible.

Agents often specialize in a particular type of property, either by choice or reputation, and just by looking at the properties advertised it becomes obvious that some sell mostly modern and lower priced property whilst others deal exclusively with the higher end of the market or in rural properties. This does not mean that specialist agents never stray from the norm, so it is still worth registering with them even if they appear to deal mostly with properties which are outside your requirements.

To get the best use of estate agents, and to ensure that a suitable property is not missed, register with as many agents as possible. Registration should be done with care to ensure the agent has a good idea of what type of property is sought, but leaving aside those aspect of a new home that are essential to you, try to be fairly flexible initially, or you will find your choice is very limited. If you say you are looking for an older-style semi, you will not get any details of terraced, detached or modern properties at all. If you say you only need three bedrooms, you may not get details of those with four. It is better to give a broad outline rather than miss out on something which in retrospect you would have considered, had you known about it.

Agents routinely ask applicants to indicate the maximum price they can afford, and ordinarily only send details of properties priced at or above this figure. Rather than giving just a maximum figure, say £70,000, ask for details of properties between £50,000 and £70,000. This way, you may find the home you want for less than you thought.

Once you know what is available, you can slim down your requirements, firmly establishing exactly what you hope to find in a property, and telling the agents so that they can help you find it. If you are consistently vague about your requirements, agents can hardly be blamed for sending details of the wrong type of property or, more importantly, not sending details of the right one.

Keep in contact with the agents you register with. They tire of sending out property details to applicants who do not give them any feedback, and you run the risk of being struck off their register if you do not give the impression of being genuinely keen to buy. If agents do not hear from you for several weeks, they will assume that you have found a property through another agency. They know that whilst applicants are keen to register, they rarely bother to advise when they are no longer looking. If agents did not slim down their applicant register regularly, they would not have time to do anything other than orchestrate the dispatch of property details. To avoid being deleted from an agent's register, you should make sure you are easily contactable, and either view properties you receive details of or let the agent know why they are not suitable.

If you report back to the agents after each viewing you will help the agents to establish a clear picture of what you are *not* looking for. Agents do not want to waste time arranging viewings which do not result in a sale, any more than you want to attend them, but if there is no response after a viewing, agents cannot be expected to hazard a guess as to why a property was not suitable.

> **TAKE A TIP**
> Back up your knowledge of what properties are for sale
> by visiting areas of particular appeal, on the look out for
> For Sale boards.

Buying without an estate agent

Using an estate agent may seem the obvious way of finding a property, but people who advertise their requirements in the local newspaper are often pleasantly surprised by the response they receive. Many newspapers have *Property Wanted* sections, and even if they don't, they will usually be pleased to run a single advertisement. Some of the sellers who respond to such an advertisement will already be marketing their property through an agent, but others will be spurred into selling when faced with a prospective buyer who is actively searching for their particular type of property. Just because a property is not already for sale does not mean the owner is not keen to sell, and if you find a property this way you have the advantage of not being in competition with anyone else.

Alternatively, you could consult the local media for 'for sale' advertisements placed by sellers. There may be an estate agent involved, in addition to the seller's own efforts, but if not, a private seller has the advantage of avoiding estate-agency fees (around 2-3% of the selling price), so you could negociate splitting this saving. If there is an agent involved, the seller will probably be tied to an agreement to pay the agency fee regardless of whether it is the seller's advertisement or the agent's endeavours which attract a buyer.

You could also use the direct approach of knocking on the doors of properties you like the look of, or posting a polite note asking if the owner might consider selling. A note is probably better. Cold calling puts the owner on the spot, and he may turn the caller away automatically, as he would a salesman or other uninvited caller. In any case, the person who answers the door may not be the best member of the household to approach, or be in a position to make a decision. If you do call personally and get a negative response, leave a note of your name and address anyway, so that the owner can get in touch if he changes his mind. You never know.

When the property market is slow, a direct approach can be fruitful. Some home owners may want to sell but do not bother to put their home on the market because they anticipate difficulty finding a buyer. Others may have previously tried to sell, then taken their property off the market because they did not find a buyer quickly. In both cases, a direct approach would be well received.

Independent negotiations without an agent are direct between buyer and seller, but you should not feel intimidated by the absence of a mediator into offering more than you would have ordinarily. Once the owner receives an offer, he may approach an estate agency for a valuation so that he knows what his property is worth. You will already know what the property is worth, both as a commodity and to you personally, and hopefully the aspirations of both parties will not be too far removed to reach a compromise.

TAKE A TIP

Aim to have the last word during price negotiations. If you make an offer which is not acceptable and the seller suggests something higher, rather than simply agreeing to this figure try to bring it down a little. If the seller won't move on price, and you still want to proceed, compromise by agreeing to his price, but only on the understanding that it includes something extra, perhaps a fitment which was not previously included.

Ordinarily the estate agent acts as go-between for buyer and seller, eliminating the need for direct contact between the two parties. However, buying without an agent necessitates some sort of relationship and it is in everyone's best interests if this relationship is cordial. You can take your lead from the seller on the degree of formality required, and will soon discover whether minor queries are best addresses through your solicitor or whether the seller is happy for you to contact him direct. You should, however, advise your solicitor of any arrangements you make with the seller.

In normal circumstances the agent who markets a property knows the seller's reason for selling (or at least thinks he does), and can advise you of the length and complexity of any 'chain' involved. This information is useful to you because it points out potential delays in the conveyance before you decide to buy, but it is not essential. Relevant facts of real importance can be obtained through your solicitor before you submit an offer, and if the offer itself comes through your solicitor this often carries more weight with the seller than a verbal offer through an estate agent.

The conveyance process is the same as when buying through an agent, although you must, in the absence of any written details from an agency, supply your solicitor with as much information about the property as possible.

Viewings

Having registered with estate agents and received a mountain of property details, and having then dismissed quite a few which are obviously unsuitable, you will probably still be left with dozens of properties which seem, on paper at least, to be likely candidates for viewing. It helps, when faced with so many properties that you hardly know where to start, to sort them into categories – those which look most suitable, those which show promise, and those which can be held in reserve if nothing comes of the others. Don't be overawed by a large number of properties to consider. The list will be slimmed down as you find out more about each one, so in the early stages it is best not to dismiss too many out of hand until you can obtain enough information to make an informed decision.

There may be one or two properties which stand out from the rest, and seem so perfect that you can hardly wait to get inside to look around. If this is the case, by all means telephone the selling agents and arrange viewings immediately. Most of the properties will not inspire such enthusiasm, and in all likelihood it will be one of these lesser candidates that turns out to be the most suitable in the end!

Don't throw away any of the written details until you have made a final choice, and preferably not until the purchase is well under way. You may need to reconsider properties which did not originally seem suitable if your priorities change whilst the search is on, if your initial selection proves disappointing, or if the purchase falls through for some reason.

Before arranging any viewing appointments, it is worth taking a look at suitable properties from the outside first, before deciding whether an internal viewing is worthwhile. Even a cursory glance will be more enlightening than the selling agent's photograph, and also enables you to find out exactly where the properties are situated and what is around them. Make a note on the agency details of anything which needs clarification, then ask the agent to find out about it before arranging a viewing.

To arrange a viewing simply contact the agent who sent the details and ask him to make an appointment with the seller. Most sellers are prepared to put themselves out to make viewings easy for potential buyers (and so they should if they want to secure a sale) so you should not experience any difficulty getting a convenient appointment. If the agent is marketing several properties which interest you, ask him to arrange a schedule of viewings, allowing enough time to view each property before travelling to the next. Each viewing will probably take around half an hour. If you do not know the area (or even if you do) the agent may be willing to arrange transport to ferry you between viewings.

Most sellers choose to conduct a viewing themselves, rather than let the selling agents handle it. Some of them are good at it, giving just the right amount of information about the property and area. Others either bombard the buyer with enthusiastic chit-chat or, at the other extreme, are downright uncommunicative. Don't be put off buying a property by the personality of the seller. He or she is not included in the price.

When arriving for a viewing try to allow enough time to drive or walk around the immediate vicinity. This gives you an opportunity to observe the comings and goings of the neighbourhood, and you could uncover something detrimental to the location, like a flight path, a lot of passing traffic or even offensive smells, which might not be evident from inside.

Looking at the property itself, do not limit your observations to an internal inspection. On arrival, take time to inspect the outside of the property as well, to take stock of the state of repair. You do not need to be a surveyor to notice neglect. Peeling paint, crumbling garden walls, loose guttering or damaged roof tiles tell more about the general condition of a property than internal decoration, which may have been tidied up with a lick of paint.

Once inside, you will probably get an instant impression which is either good or bad and you may well decide that a property is not for you within a few seconds of entering it. If you feel immediately negative about a property it is probably worth trusting your instincts, although bear in mind that you could be dismissing a basically sound and suitable property just because the decoration is outdated or not to your taste. Obviously if complete redecorating is necessary the cost would need to be built into your purchasing budget, and if professional decorators are called in this could be a hefty sum, but ultimately the suitability of the accommodation and location are more important than what colour the wallpaper is.

If you feel immediately positive about a property, be less trusting. It is easy to be so bowled over by aesthetics that other more important things get overlooked, so unless you have satisfied your basic criteria and can honestly say that your feelings are practical as well as emotional, be cautious about making a hasty decision.

Aim to find out as much as possible during a viewing. Firstly, look around carefully. Don't limit your observations to a quick glance taking more notice of the current owner's furniture and effects than of the accommodation itself. Look at the proportions of each room. Would your furniture fit? Look at the general condition. Is it sound? What is the state of the ceilings – are they water-stained or cracked? Then consider the decoration; not just whether you like it, but more importantly whether there are any tell-tale signs of damp or disrepair. When looking out of the windows to take in the view, look at the frames as well, and note if condensation is a problem. Major defects will be unearthed by employing a professional surveyor, but most survey reports do not mention every defect, and discovering at the viewing stage something which makes the property unsuitable for you could avoid a waste of time and money in the long run.

> **TOP TIP**
> If all the neighbouring properties have replaced their roof tiles, you can reasonably assume that you might have to do the same fairly soon.

The structure of each viewing (whether it starts with the outside or inside, upstairs or downstairs) depends to a large extent on the seller, since he is the one who conducts the 'tour'. How long the viewing takes will also depend on the seller. If he or she is chatty, you may find yourself detained indefinitely in each room as its attributes are expansively detailed. Prolonged viewings can be exhausting, but are at least informative. Short viewings are a waste of time if you do not get the opportunity to see all you need. It might be that the seller does not like showing strangers round his home, and who can blame him, or it might be that he simply isn't very good at conducting viewings; but if a particular aspect is important to you, don't be put off asking about it. Rarely are prospective buyers rushed through a property because the seller is not that keen to sell. It is more likely that he hopes your attention will not be drawn to anything detrimental if the tour is brief.

Whilst progressing from room to room, you will be able to establish exactly what fixtures and fittings are included in the purchase price, which may greatly influence the amount you are prepared to pay, or even the decision to buy at all.

Don't be afraid to ask questions and request to see anything which is not immediately apparent, such as roof insulation or the workings of the boiler. You may want information about running costs, so if this is important to you be sure to get factual evidence in the form of copy bills for at least the past year, to give a realistic overview. Don't rely on the seller's verbal assurance that the bills are 'quite low'.

Don't despair if you like a property but do not feel you know enough about it after a viewing to make a decision. If you have specific queries the agent should be able to supply you with some answers, and a second viewing (highly recommended even if you think you have seen enough of the property to make a positive decision after one visit) refreshes the memory if a great many viewings have led to some confusion.

If the seller mentions any treatments performed on the property, perhaps against damp or wood infestation, be sure to ask your solicitor to obtain the guarantees if you decide to go ahead with the purchase.

If the property has been the subject of building work, such as the addition of a new garage or extension, the seller will need to supply documented evidence that the work was consented to and approved by the planning and building departments of the local authority. If building work does not have planning permission, the local authority is empowered to demand its removal, or alternatively the new owner of the property may be faced with the need to apply for retrospective planning permission which there is no guarantee he will be granted.

If the property is a leasehold, it is best to find out if there are any unacceptable restrictions in the lease, before wasting time on a viewing. The selling agent should have access to this information, or at least be able to find out about it.

TOP TIP
To get honest information from the seller, phrase questions that do not elicit Yes or No answers. If asked 'Are there plenty of restaurants in the town?' the seller is bound to say 'Yes' because that is obviously the answer you are looking for. If asked 'What restaurants are there in the town?' he has to be more specific.

You may have quite a few properties to view, all of them very similar, which can become confusing. After half a dozen appointments, the first few viewings fade to a distant memory, and the more viewings you attend the more difficult it becomes to remember what each property had to offer. To help avoid this, it is useful to jot down anything specific which occurs at the time of the viewing. The agency details will already give basic information, but they cannot cover everything. Something along the lines of the following example, marking relevant points on a scale of 1-5, or else simply scribbling a few notes on the agency details, can avoid a lot of confusion later.

ADDRESS: Mill View

	RATING	COMMENTS
Suitability of location	3	20 minutes from station
Outside appearance	5	New windows + repainted
Garden	4	large, low-maintenance
Internal decoration	2	Old but good quality
Cupboard space	5	Plenty plus loft space
Heating	5	CH plus 2 open fires

NOTES: Nice country house. Good sized rooms – plenty of light. Owners selling to move nearer daughter – keen to negotiate and able to vacate quickly. No garage but parking not a problem. Very quiet.

Making notes like this not only serves as a reminder long after the event, but also helps you to focus on what you saw at the time of the viewing.

TAKE A TIP
Look at the type of neighbours you will inherit. They will tell you almost as much about an area as the properties themselves.

Lastly, try to find out during a viewing how motivated the seller is. Has he found a new home to move to? How quickly does he plan to move out once he finds a buyer? He may be buying a new home which is nowhere near completion. The selling agents usually know their client's plans, but remember that their first loyalty is to the paying customer, so do not expect a good agent to divulge information which could be detrimental to the sale. He may not want to tell you something which could put you off – but this is exactly the information you need to avoid making a wrong decision.

TAKE A TIP

In an uncertain property market, a seller who accepts a low offer may have second thoughts and pull out of the sale if he thinks he could sell for more in a few months' time.

Many people feel obliged to put on a poker face during viewings, especially if they like the property, fearing any show of enthusiasm could push the price up. In reality, a seller is probably more likely to negotiate with someone who seems keen to buy than he is with someone whose 'take it or leave it' attitude inspires little confidence that negotiations will result in a sale. On the other hand, there is no need to pretend that you like a particular property if you do not. You may discover immediately on arrival for a viewing that some aspect of the building itself or its location makes it unsuitable. When this happens it is easier, and kinder to the seller, to confess on the doorstep that the viewing would not be worthwhile, rather than wasting everyone's time traipsing round a property with absolutely no intention of buying it.

Second viewings

It is essential to view a second time those properties which evoke enthusiasm, before making a final decision. Curiously, most people like a property less the second time they view it, so don't be surprised if a return visit fails to impress as much as the first.

If the seller was uncommunicative during the initial viewing, calling a second time might be more conducive to conversation because the atmosphere is usually less formal. The seller feels confident that the stranger he is allowing into his home is seriously considering buying it, and you will feel more comfortable in surroundings which are now familiar. Often during a second viewing, buyers are encouraged to view at their own pace, unsupervised, which gives them the opportunity to look around without distraction.

Sellers sometimes see a second viewing as indication that the sale is in the bag, which could be embarrassing for you if you are also viewing several other properties a second time before making up your mind. Honesty is probably the best policy here, with a good measure of tact and diplomacy thrown in. If the seller starts discussing moving dates, or suggests inviting the neighbours in for introductions, you would do well to point out gently that you have one or two other properties to see again before making a firm decision.

TOP TIP
If a property is well liked but one or two minor flaws cast doubt on its suitability, it is worth approaching the seller or selling agents to see if a solution can be found. At worst, they can only say no, and it costs nothing to ask.

A second viewing is usually less emotionally driven. You will already know what the property has to offer, and can now take a really good look at the building itself with a clear head. Common sense and observation can reveal major structural defects or costly repairs – it is unnecessary and expensive for a surveyor to put in black and white what your eyes are already telling you.

Moving to a new area
Finding the right property can be tedious at the best of times, but relocating to an unfamiliar area brings added complications, like not knowing local property values, or about available transport, schools etc., and ignorance of the most desirable locations and those best avoided. There is also a risk, when moving to a completely different part of the country, that you could be rushed into making a decision simply because journeying to view properties is so time-consuming. However, it is

possible to do a lot of homework before getting to the stage of trundling up the motorway to view individual properties, saving a great deal of time.

First things first. Get hold of a telephone directory for the area you are moving to (Yellow Pages or similar) and a copy of a local newspaper with a property section. These give details of estate agents who operate in the area so that you can register as a potential buyer without leaving the comfort of your armchair. Rather than telephoning the agents, it might be simpler to write a letter explaining that you are moving to the area, listing the requirements you need of your new home (price range, type of property sought etc.) and then send a photocopy to all the local agents. This saves repeating yourself over the telephone and keeps the phone bill down.

If you are keen to get details of available properties quickly, there is nothing else for it but to visit personally all the agents in the area. You can then speak to them direct about your requirements and collect details of any properties which seem suitable. Whilst in the agents' office, you can also get some verbal information about the area, and might also be offered a local map.

Whilst you will probably know in advance roughly what type of property you are looking for, you should not at this stage be too rigid when giving your requirements to agents, at least until you know what type of property is available.

Look through the local paper to get an idea of current prices in the area. This helps to put your expectations into proportion, since at the time of registration you need to decide roughly how much you want to spend. Property prices in different parts of the country vary enormously, so prepare for either a pleasant surprise or a nasty shock.

Before starting to plough through the agency details it is helpful, if not essential, to have a map of the town or area so that you can see where each property is situated. You can then begin to familiarize yourself with the peculiarities of each part of the town or locality. You may notice, for example, that a large proportion of properties for sale are in the same streets or estates, indicating a dense and transient population. Other more sought-after areas will be easily identified as those where property rarely comes on the market, and of course the prices will usually be higher. A map will also be invaluable when you come to arrange a schedule of viewings, helping you to plan a route to visit one property after another without criss-crossing the area needlessly or allowing too little or too much time to get from one viewing to another.

If newly built homes are of interest to you, there are many house-building projects up and down the country so you will probably have several sites to choose from. The builders sometimes sell direct to the public, advertising in the local media, or alternatively may hand the marketing over to estate agents, in which case it is worth mentioning when registering with agents that you would like details of new homes as well as established properties. It is also possible to contact the building companies direct by telephoning or writing to their regional offices (directory enquiries should be able to give you the telephone numbers) and they will then be able to advise of any sites in the area you are moving to.

Ultimately you will visit the area yourself, and it may be worthwhile staying for a long weekend which will give you time to familiarize yourself with the area. This is especially useful if you are not tied to moving to a particular town but have the choice of several. The more choice you have, the longer it will take to explore. When visiting, either to look around or attend viewings, bear the following in mind:

- Give yourself enough time to get a feel for the area. Talk to the 'natives' – are they friendly and enthusiastic about their town? In rural areas, time spent in the local pub can be profitable, allowing you to glean valuable information about the surrounding villages and what amenities each has to recommend it, and is a pleasurable exercise in itself.
- Take time to walk around the town or just sit on a bench and watch the comings and goings – you can learn a lot from simply observing your surroundings so trust your instincts. Does the town centre seem to be thriving with plenty of activity, or have a lot of the shops closed down? Look carefully at the people, and you will usually get some idea of the predominant age-group and social condition of the population.

- Find out if your interests are catered for, e.g. whether there are restaurants, cinemas etc.; and, if you have children, what schools are available, what they are like and where they are situated.
- Visit the local tourist information office if there is one, and pick up any available literature on the area. The local library may also have some useful information.
- If you are moving with your job, ask your new colleagues which areas they recommend, but allow for the fact that what they like may not be what you like. Personal opinions vary, but if you speak to enough people you begin to get a picture of how the area is arranged and what it has to offer.

TAKE A TIP
If you will be travelling to work, test the route
(preferably during the rush hour) to see how long it takes.
This can be deceptive and sometimes a trip across a town
can take up more precious minutes that a journey from
a village, which may involve more mileage but less
traffic congestion.

A lack of local knowledge makes second viewings even more important than usual, not only to double check that a specific property is right for your but also to look at the street and general area at different times of the day and preferably on different days of the week. You do not want to buy a home in what appears at first sight to be a quiet cul-de-sac only to discover that it becomes a playground for noisy children when the school day is over.

As a final note, an *ineffective* way of searching for property in an unknown area is by driving around aimlessly looking for estate agency *For Sale* boards. Some properties which are for sale may not have a *For Sale* board, and those which do give little indication from the outside of the accommodation inside.

Submitting an offer

Once the right property has been found, it is time to start negotiating the price. In this day and age a property rarely sells at the advertised price, so in most cases you can ignore the estate agent's valuation and decide for yourself what a property is currently, worth, i.e. what you think *you* could sell it for. The only time to take notice of a selling price is if it is low, but if you do not know current values, you will not spot a genuine bargain. If you become a conscientious observer of the property market BEFORE starting the hunt for your new home, you will be well versed in local price trends. Don't be shy of offering less than the advertised selling price – the vendor may refuse your offer, but it's worth a try.

Current market value is not the only consideration in determining how much to offer. You must also decide what the property is worth to you personally. You may feel so passionately about a particular property that you are happy to pay an inflated price because to you the property is worth almost any amount. The problem is that you will loose money if you cannot find an equally enthusiastic buyer when trying to sell the property yourself in the future. If you like a property but not the price, you should only offer what it is worth to you, and no more.

Often, during viewings, sellers intimate directly or indirectly what amount they are looking to obtain. They may indicate that several previous offers have already been refused because they were too low, or else say that someone else is 'interested in buying' once they can proceed. Some sellers even make it clear that they are not prepared to accept any offers lower than the asking price, especially if their property has only recently come on to the market. However, in a few months they will probably be desperate enough to reconsider. The best advice is to ignore whatever sellers say concerning price, and judge for yourself what to offer. The sellers might well have an interested party waiting in the wings, but they could be waiting a very long time. Even if they want to decline the first few offers to see what maximum they can get, you, the buyer, should still only offer what the property is worth to you.

There are property bargains to be found for those who are prepared to haggle over the price. An initial offer might well be accepted, but if not, you can usually increase it until you find the seller's bottom line. Reducing an offer after it has been accepted is not so easy, and causes a bad relationship between buyer and seller.

Offers are usually made through the selling agent, verbally in the first instance, or to the seller direct. An offer is not binding until contracts are exchanged, but it should be stated that the offer is 'Subject to Survey and Contract'. You can make an offer and then retract it, or reduce it if you feel so inclined, perhaps because a subsequent survey puts a lower value on the property than the offer figure, or else a flaw in the building comes to light which reduced its worth to you. In such cases you might decide to withdraw from the purchase altogether, or you might reduce your offer to take account of the changed circumstances.

Such is the risk of a buyer withdrawing his offer (a property can be 'sold' several times before finally completing a sale) that wise sellers leave their property on the market until contracts are exchanged. By so doing, the property continues to be advertised and any interested buyers are held in reserve in case the original sale falls through. If a property is 'under offer' but still open to viewing until contracts are exchanged, the selling agents either keep to themselves the amount of the offer in the hope that any subsequent ones are higher, or else they let potential buyers know the amount of the offer so that they do not waste time offering less. Occasionally a subsequent offer of the same amount or even slightly lower is accepted from someone in a better buying position, but more commonly a property with wide appeal attracts ever higher offers, each now one 'gazumping' the last.

To protect against being gazumped, it helps to present yourself as a serious buyer in a position to proceed with the purchase quickly, so you should arrange your mortgage funding in principle before making an offer and do everything in your power to keep the administration moving smoothly. Chapter 6 gives some advice on how to work with your solicitor to help him complete the legal conveyance quickly, and you may need to badger your lender and surveyor to avoid delays. In addition, you could obtain from your solicitor (or direct from the RICS by telephoning 0171 222 7000) a 'standard personal contract' which aims to stop gazumping by tying both seller and buyer to the purchase once an offer has been accepted.

When a seller considers whether or not to accept an offer, he usually has in mind a minimum sum he can afford to accept, and a higher figure which is a bit optimistic. If he is buying a subsequent property, he will need to raise enough from his sale to fund the purchase, although if he receives an offer which is less than he needs, he may be able to pass on the loss, or part of it, by reducing his own offer.

It is not unheard of for a buyer who has not yet sold his current home to make an offer on the next one, then reduce that offer once he finds a buyer himself and his buying position is thus improved. This ploy only works if no one else enters the arena before contracts are exchanged. The seller may refuse the lower offer if he can afford to withdraw and wait for a better offer, or is brave enough to call the buyer's bluff. And he may have no choice but to refuse if he has chosen his next home on the basis of the amount he expected to sell for.

If you make an offer which the seller refuses, it may be possible to reach a compromise which both buyer and seller can live with, over fixtures and fittings. For example, the seller may agree to your offer on the understanding that carpets and curtains are not included in the price, or else you might increase your offer on the understanding that they are.

Apart from the amount of the offer, the seller will also consider whether you can move quickly, and will usually look more favourably on an offer from someone who is not dependent on selling his own property first.

The selling agents will not (or should not) divulge how much they feel the seller is willing to accept, although they may indicate that he or she is 'open to offers', in the hope of encouraging bids. They may also encourage offers below the asking price of properties they feel are overpriced, thereby showing the sellers from the offers received what their property is really worth, and eventually securing a sale.

When you make an offer, leave some room for negotiation. If your first offer is the maximum you can afford, or the most you consider the property is worth, you cannot increase if even if you would like to. A word of warning, though: sellers can feel insulted by a low offer, and if they receive a better one (which is likely if yours is very low), they may accept this before you have a chance to suggest an increase. Even in a slow market most sellers are determined to get a good price and are rarely as desperate to sell as you might like to imagine.

Finally, if your chosen property is in need of repair or modernization, or if it would only meet your requirements after some sort of conversion, you need to calculate very carefully the cost of necessary work before deciding how much to offer. Unless you have experience of this, it is best to obtain detailed quotes for the work (or ask the seller to do so), to avoid any unpleasant surprises later. The cost of improvements can be much more than anticipated. Charges for fitting, plumbing, electrical work, carpentry etc. etc. will be on top of the price of, for example, a new kitchen, doubling the total cost of the project. You would also need to check whether planning permission is required, and if so, be sure that it would be granted.

Submitting an offer in Scotland

The process of property buying in Scotland (except for a newly built property) is different from that in England and Wales, especially when it comes to submitting an offer. Once you make a formal, conditional, offer or 'bid' which the seller accepts, agreement on any conditions is usually reached within a few days (this can happen on the day the offer is made and accepted). You and the seller are then both committed to the transaction at the agreed price, which means you cannot later reduce your offer, and the seller cannot accept a subsequent offer from someone else, without being in breach of contract.

Properties which are not new are usually advertised for sale at around the seller's minimum anticipated price, and 'offers over' that price are invited. When there is sufficient interest, the selling agent sets a closing date, by which prospective buyers must submit their 'best offers'. As a buyer you will normally have only one opportunity to make an offer, and you are bidding blind because you do not know what other interested parties are offering. If a closing date is not set, you may be able to negotiate with the seller.

You will need to make any necessary borrowing arrangements and have a valuation or survey (or both) carried out in advance, so that if your offer is accepted there are no delays. Having the survey or valuation done in advance puts you in an informed position when considering how much the property is worth, but the disadvantage is that you may have to instruct and pay for more than one survey before you make an offer which is successful.

The procedure for buying homes and conveyancing in Scotland is covered in more detail in Chapter 7.

Chains

In England and Wales, sale and purchase transactions often fail to reach completion through no fault of the seller or buyer, but simply because the 'chain' which each finds himself in breaks down. A 'chain' is the term used to describe a series of simultaneous transactions involving more than one buyer and seller, likening them to links in a chain. For example:

A has nothing to sell and is buying from B
B is buying from C
C is buying from D
D is buying a newly built home

If any one of the 'links' pulls out of the chain, the whole series of transactions can break down. If, for example, C withdraws because he cannot raise sufficient funds to buy from D, this leaves his buyer (B) with no property to buy, and the person he was buying from (D) with no buyer. In cases like this, the end of the chain is irrevocably broken because D has to start all over again in his search for a buyer before he can purchase his new home. The bottom of the chain could be saved if B is able to find another property to buy quickly, but if he takes too long his buyer (A) could decide to buy somewhere else. If the first-time buyer (A) backs out, the chain could stay intact, but only if the rest of the 'links' are prepared to wait for B to find another buyer.

This example is a fairly small chain with only four links so it would stand a good chance of success. Because so many failed purchases are the result of broken chains, you might like to find out about the length and complexity of the chain you would become involved before making an offer on a particular property. If it is very long or is showing signs of difficulty, this could reflect your decision to buy. The selling agents are usually able to advise how many transactions are involved and whether there are any weak links.

TAKE A TIP

If the person you are buying from is moving to a property in the process of being built, make sure that exchange and completion will go ahead as arranged, whether or not the new property is completed on schedule. In the winter months especially, weather conditions can hinder construction, leading to considerable delay for those further down the chain. Do not sign a contract without a fixed completion date unless you are prepared to move into temporary accommodation.

Buying positions

Sometimes a seller's decision whether or not to accept an offer, especially if it is low, is based on how quickly the buyer can complete the purchase. Buyers usually fall into one of four categories, depending on their 'buying position' or ability to proceed with a purchase without delay. In descending order of popularity, these are:

• First time buyer

This buyer has nothing to sell so he is in an excellent bargaining position. Assuming his funding has been arranged, he can proceed with the purchase without delay.

• **Own property sold**

The buyer's present property has been sold. This could mean that the buyer has actually moved out of his property into temporary accommodation, or alternatively that contracts have been exchanged and he is just waiting for the finalities to be concluded. Either way, the buyer has in effect disposed of his property and is in a position to purchase without delay. This type of buyer can probably drive a hard bargain, since he knows that few other buyers will be in as good a position as he, and his custom is therefore sought after.

If the buyer has not actually vacated his current property, but this is imminent, he might insist that the purchase transaction fits in with his sale (conveyance procedures permitting), instead of getting tied up in a chain, in an attempt to avoid a timing problem which could force him to vacate with nowhere to move into.

• **Sold subject to contract**

This buyer has received an offer on his own property but has yet to exchange contracts, so there is still an element of doubt over whether his sale is secure. The length of chain he is already involved in may be considered before any offer he makes is accepted. His bargaining position is not very strong at this point, but if he waits until contracts are exchanged on his own sale before submitting an offer, he improves his bargaining position by moving into the 'sold' category above.

• **On the market, but not yet sold**

This buyer is in exactly the same position as the person he is buying from. His buying status does not lend itself to bargaining over price, since it could take him longer to get an offer on his own property than for the seller to find another buyer. If this buyer's offer is accepted in principle, the property will almost certainly remain on the market, in case someone in a better buying position comes along.

Surveys and valuations

All property purchases which rely on funding from banks or building societies have to be inspected by a surveyor before the lenders will part with any money. Since the property is the lenders' security, he needs to be sure it is worth at least the amount being lent, so that the loan can easily be recouped in the event of repossession. The lender has a duty to himself (and arguably to his client) to ensure that the purchase is a sound investment, but as a borrower/buyer you should not assume that a lender's mortgage offer suggests the property is worth the purchase price or that it is in reasonable condition. Although it is the lender who insists on the surveyor's report, it is the borrower/buyer who pays for it.

The surveyor has two main functions when submitting his report. Firstly he checks that the property is in the condition it appears to be, bringing defects to the attention of the buyer and lender. Secondly, he gives his opinion on the value of the property, giving the lender and buyer an indication of what amount the property could raise on disposal, should the need arise.

You should already have looked carefully at the property you want to buy, and taken note of any obvious faults, but an experienced surveyor ought to discover any major defects in the building which you might have missed. However, you should not rely too heavily on a surveyor to protect your interests, especially if the inspection is a basic Lender's Valuation Report. This, as the name suggests, is generally concerned with valuing the property from the lender's point of view, and not with unearthing defects which might affect the living conditions or appearance of the property, which will be just as important to you. Even a comprehensive survey may not be conclusive. It will comment on serious decay or damage in the fabric of the building, but minor flaws might not be worthy of mention.

The extent of the surveyor's inspection is often limited by the access he is able to obtain, since fitted carpets and fitted furniture may be restrictive when it comes to inspecting floorboards and sections of wall etc. If the surveyor is unable to access certain areas of the property, his report will usually say so. If you have a particular query regarding the property you may be able to ask the surveyor to look at this specifically, although the flexibility of the report depends on the type of report commissioned, or to put it bluntly, how much the surveyor is being paid.

The value of a surveyor's report cannot be denied, and many buyers have been saved the expense and disruption of huge repairs because their surveyor pointed out defects which they themselves had not noticed. However, it is a mistake to assume that surveyors report on every tiny defect in a property, or to treat the report as insurance against any future defects. The surveyor can only comment on the condition of the property at the time of his inspection. He may, for example, report that the roof is in good condition, and can hardly be held responsible if a heavy storm some months after the purchase loosens several roof tiles sufficiently to allow water penetration which then results in damage.

Surveyors are qualified people who mostly know what they are doing and go about their work diligently. To protect themselves against those who would unfairly lay blame at their feet, most inspection reports carry some sort of 'disclaimer' to explain exactly what the report covers (which is precious little in the case of a valuation report) and what it does not. The 'valuation' report is perhaps inappropriately named because, without the benefit of conducting a comprehensive inspection of the condition of the property, is the surveyor in a position to consider its value accurately?

Which survey to choose

Lenders usually appoint a surveyor of their choosing, but you will be able to select the level of inspection, depending on the amount of information you hope to gain from the report, and the price you are willing to pay for it. There are basically four different types of 'survey':

• Lender's Valuation Report

This is primarily a valuation of the property to ensure it provides adequate security for the loan (or mortgage) being made on it. The value of the property needs at least to equal the amount the buyer needs to raise by mortgage. The surveyor does not normally lift floorboards or delve too deeply into the fabric of the property during a Valuation, but he may advise obtaining a further specialist report if he feels this would be appropriate. He will report on 'essential repairs' which, if left uncorrected, would cause further damage to the property, and comment on specific aspects of the property's condition which has led to his valuation. Individual defects mentioned tend to be only those which reflect on the value. Other defects, although they would involve repair costs, may not be mentioned.

• Home Buyer's Survey and Valuation

This type of report will almost certainly give the surveyor's considered opinion regarding the value of the property at that time, and provide information on factors which might influence its future value. The surveyor may, when assessing value, comment on current market conditions which could affect the selling price. This type of report is more in-depth than a straight Valuation, and gives details of the property's general condition, often mentioning specific defects. However, because it is usually prepared on pre-printed forms, it does not allow much flexibility for comment on any particular queries you may have.

• Building Report

Sometimes referred to as a structural survey, this type of report is the most extensive, and is sometimes the second step if a Valuation or Home Buyer's Survey recommends that more detailed information is needed before the purchase goes ahead. The report is usually commissioned by the buyer and is rather costly, but its advantage is that it enables you to raise any specific queries with the surveyor. Services are commented on where visible, although they probably won't be physically tested by the surveyor. Specialists in heating, drainage, etc. may be called in to supply additional reports if required. The surveyor often requests details of any charges (ground rent, council taxes etc.) relating to the property, along with details of boundaries. He also comments on any building repairs or alterations which could affect the property and the likely cost of remedial work to correct faults. Considering the cost of this type of report, make sure you know what you will get for your money. Minor defects such as loose door fittings or cracked glass are not usually mentioned, but the general condition of the property will be appraised, including the following:

- foundations
- walls, both external and internal
- internal flooring and ceilings
- windows, doors and external joinery
- fascia and soffit boards
- pipes, drains and gutters
- roof
- chimney stacks

The results of a valuation or survey may directly affect whether or not the buyer goes ahead with the purchase. Not only that, it also determines the amount your lender will be prepared to lend and can affect the final purchase price if you can use the report as a bargaining tool. Once you have a surveyor's report on a property and its condition, you are in a position to haggle over the price and may negotiate a reduction in view of any necessary repairs, even though the selling agent's initial marketing valuation may have already taken these into account.

The valuation figure arrived at by a surveyor may be less than your original offer, in which case you could reasonably reduce it, especially if you are borrowing a large proportion of the purchase price. In any event, be guided by the surveyor concerning value, and it would be unwise to pay much more for a property than the surveyor considers it is worth.

> **DID YOU KNOW?** *A local surveyor usually has a good knowledge of market prices and is often a better judge of a property's value than the selling agents. Unlike the agents, he is not under pressure to meet the sellers' price aspirations, and can give a totally honest valuation.*

The results of a survey or valuation can make or break a property sale, and the sale could fall through if the report is unfavourable. Given this, the sellers of the home you are buying may wait for the results of your survey on their property before going to the expense of paying for a survey on their own purchase, just in case the sale to you does not go ahead. This is an understandable practice, but obviously causes delay. It could also be an indication that the seller *expects* a surveyor to find something wrong with his property.

For surveys and valuations in Scotland, refer to *Buying in Scotland*, Chapter 7.

Surveys on leasehold properties

As with the purchase of a freehold property, if you are borrowing money to buy a leasehold (usually a flat), your lender will require a survey and/or valuation report before granting a mortgage. Unlike the survey of a freehold property, however, the survey of a leasehold property will consider parts of the building not directly included in the purchase, because the condition of the whole building is relevant. As a leaseholder, you will be contributing to the maintenance and repair of areas outside your four walls, and the general condition of the whole building affects the value of an individual flat.

Costs

The cost of a surveyor's report is usually based on the value of the property; the more expensive the property, the more expensive the report. Lenders usually print on their promotional material the scale of fees their borrowers are charged if the report is commissioned through them. Although the buyer pays for the report, he does not usually receive a copy of it as a matter of course. However, a polite request to the lender usually results in a copy being sent.

Fees for privately arranged surveys vary across the country. Different firms of surveyors have their own rates, and provide quotations on request. Naturally a comprehensive appraisal of a property costs more than a basic valuation, so a Building Report will be considerably more expensive than a Home Buyer's Survey, which in turn will be more expensive than a Mortgage Valuation.

Do you need a surveyor's report?

Undoubtedly, yes. Apart from the fact that your lender will insist on one, it would be foolish to make such a large purchase without so much as a second opinion on its condition and value.

My own personal observation on survey reports, for what it's worth, is thus. The most popular middle-of-the-road survey, the Home Buyer's Survey, the type highly recommended by lenders, costs a tidy sum for something which is often sadly inconclusive. You might just as well go for the basic lender's valuation which is similarly vague but costs less. If you want a thorough inspection, there is nothing else for it but to stomach the high cost of a full buildings or structural survey. No report is foolproof, but at least this type of inspection goes further than simply reporting on what most reasonably observant buyers would notice anyway, and you can usually ask to be present during the inspection to raise any specific queries at the time.

2. FINANCING A PURCHASE

Unless you are fortunate enough to have sufficient cash to buy a home outright, you will need to arrange some form of loan to fund the purchase. Most buyers do this by means of a mortgage with a bank or building society.

What is a mortgage?

How does a mortgage work? Basically the lender (or *mortgagee*, e.g. bank or building society) grants the borrower (the *mortgagor*) a sum of money for the purchase of a property. The borrower (you) agrees to repay the loan and interest over a specified period (the term – commonly 25 years but it is possible to arrange a term of between 10 and 35 years), during which time the lender holds the property as security. This means the lender can take possession of the property and sell it in order to settle the outstanding debt if the borrower fails to keep up the repayment schedule. You are allowed to occupy the property or sell it at any time during the term of the mortgage, but the deeds are held by the lender and you do not become the sole owner of the property until the loan and interest have been fully paid.

The property is the lender's security on the money loaned until the mortgage is repaid, but any increase in the value of the property belongs to you. Whilst the monthly repayment amounts may fluctuate as a result of changes to the prevailing interest rate (although not for fixed-rate mortgages), the capital amount owed cannot be increased.

If you sell the property before the end of the mortgage term, the proceeds of the sale are used to pay back the amount remaining on loan, redeeming the mortgage. If the property is sold for more than you borrowed, the extra money belongs to you, but if the property is sold for less than the outstanding loan, you will need to make up the difference to pay off the mortgage. Since the property crash of the 1980s and 1990s, many borrowers have found themselves in this position, i.e. their property has dropped in value so that it is now worth less than the loan secured on it. This distressing state of affairs has become known as 'negative equity' (see below).

If you wish, you can usually transfer your mortgage to another lender, and you may choose to do this if a different lender offers a better arrangement, although any financial inducement already enjoyed will have to be paid back, and an early redemption charge may be payable.

TOP TIP
'Re-mortgaging' can be a way of reducing monthly repayments, by extending the term of the existing loan.

Where to go for a mortgage

With so many institutions advertising mortgage lending, the choice of who to approach for funding can be baffling. With such a wide choice, you are almost certain to find the right mortgage eventually, but it does mean wading through a great deal of promotional literature to get all the facts before making a commitment. It is crucial not to be rushed into the wrong type of mortgage, so take your time choosing the right one. This is one of the reasons it is better to arrange funding provisionally before starting to look for your new home. If you do it the other way round, enthusiasm to move in quickly could force a hasty decision.

Lenders can be approached direct. You can request an appointment to speak with the mortgage advisor or manager who then explains in detail the various mortgages offered and any special deals available at the time. If you already have an account with a bank or building society, you might prefer to keep all your financial affairs with one institution, but it does no harm to shop around first, especially since lenders do not necessarily give preferential treatment to existing customers. If anything, it seems they are at pains to attract new custom rather than work to retain existing clients.

Alternatively, you could approach a mortgage broker. The broker assesses your lending requirements and then, with his knowledge of mortgages available from various lenders, helps you select what seems to be the right one for you. Mortgage brokers do not generally charge a fee for finding you a suitable mortgage. They get their commission from the sale of mortgage-related policies, paid by the suppliers of the 'product'. Independent mortgage brokers and financial advisers are required to offer the best advice applicable to each individual, so they should not be biased in favour of any particular lender. The advantage of using a broker is that he has knowledge of many lenders, whereas a particular bank or building society does not, and is hardly likely to recommend products offered by a competitor in preference his own.

How much can you borrow?

Your lenders will take account of your salary when calculating the amount they feel you can reasonably afford to repay. They will usually lend up to 3 times your annual salary and the amount of the second salary if the purchase is a joint one, or $2^1/_2$ times the combined annual salary. If you are self employed, your lenders may contact your accountant for income details.

The percentage of the purchase price a lender will fund varies between institutions. It is possible to borrow 100% of the purchase price (or even more – see *Negative equity*, below), but more commonly the maximum lending percentage is 75-95%, so you will still need to contribute part of the purchase price.

Example: If your annual salary is £11,000 and your partner's is £9,000, and the lenders agree to fund $2^1/_2$ times the joint annual income, the maximum mortgage funding available based on income is £50,000. However, if the property you want to buy costs £50,000, you cannot usually borrow all of it but only, say, 75% of the purchase price, i.e. £37,500.

The amount you can borrow will also depend on the result of the surveyor's valuation. If the lenders' borrowing percentage is a maximum 75%, they will only lend 75% of the surveyor's valuation. In other words, if the surveyor values the property at, say, £47,000, but you have offered the seller £50,000, the lenders will not usually lend more than 75% of

£47,000. You could stand by your offer of £50,000 if you can afford to make up the difference, but naturally the surveyor's report gives grounds for negotiation.

If you apply for a loan greater than 75% of the purchase price or valuation (whichever is lower), you may be charged an MGI (Mortgage Guarantee Insurance) fee.

DID YOU KNOW? *If you are buying a plot of land to build on, you can take out a mortgage on the land, but not the cost of building the property. This is because until the building is completed, there is nothing to secure the loan on.*

Lenders limit the amount they lend to what, in their experience, they feel borrowers can generally afford to borrow. Your lenders' concern will be that you keep to the repayment schedule, but they cannot be fully aware of your lifestyle or how much cash you need to maintain that lifestyle. Neither can the lenders judge what future financial commitments you may face. It is therefore up to you to satisfy yourself that you can afford to meet the monthly repayments, and not rely entirely on the lenders' opinion of your financial commitments.

Work out a simple income and expenditure budget. Bear in mind that a rise in interest rates will increase repayments, and allow some leeway for this and any other unforeseen rise in living costs. The pleasure of owning your own home inevitably brings with it the financial drain of maintenance and repairs, so remember to allow a float in the budget to cover this. Even a minor unexpected bill, like a plumber's charge to repair the washing machine, can put you in dire straits if your mortgage repayments are higher than you can comfortably afford. First time buyers especially should be realistic in their budget calculations, especially if they are not accustomed to paying household bills.

When calculating expenditure, you must allow for *everything*, including:

Mortgage repayments
Endowment policy (if applicable; see below)
Payment protection policy (if applicable; see below)
Personal pension
Health Insurance (if applicable)
Council tax
Electricity and gas
Telephone
Water
TV licence
Car expenses, i.e. insurance, road tax, running costs
Other transport costs
Insurance (life, building and contents insurance)
Food and clothing
Pet food/vet bills
Entertainment
Loans/HP
Credit cards
Miscellaneous
Other

The miscellaneous figure is important. It allows for cash which slips through your fingers without your really knowing where it went.

Once you have calculated your expenditure, being honest and accurate, deduct this from your income. Use your current income, without assuming it will rise in the future. It may not, but your monthly repayments and living costs might. If your income barely covers your outgoings, you do not have a financial safety net to cover any unexpected demands on your purse. You might be able to tighten your belt on food and clothing bills, or do without a car, but probably it is better to take out a smaller mortgage.

Consult a mortgage lender *before* starting to look for a property. By so doing you will know in principle how much you can borrow and the maximum you can afford to offer.

Interest rates

Interest rates vary between lenders, so it is worth shopping around for the best deals available at the time. Unless the rate is fixed (see below), the interest charged by lenders is variable, which means the rate goes up and down according to market rates at the time, increasing or decreasing your monthly repayments accordingly.

Financial institutions such as banks and building societies decide their own interest rates for borrowers and savers. They usually charge a larger interest rate to borrowers than they pay to savers. Logically they have to do this, otherwise they could not remain in business for long.

Fluctuations in interest rates charged by lenders are influenced by the Bank of England raising or lowering its interest rate. The Chancellor of the Exchequer and the Governor of the Bank of England make changes to the interest rate in an effort to control the economy of the country. When the Bank of England changes its interest rate, other banks and building societies raise or lower theirs, although they do not have to keep strictly in line with the Bank of England rate, and some act more quickly than others in putting the changes into effect.

When the rate changes (and you can be fairly certain of fluctuations during the term of a mortgage), lenders usually write to customers advising them of the amended monthly repayment figure and the date the change comes into effect.

In mortgage and other loan advertisements and on promotional literature, lenders quote two interest rates. The first is the actual rate charged on the loan. The second (often in smaller print and invariably higher) is the Annual Percentage Rate (APR), which is the total cost you will pay, taking account of the term of the loan and any administration and other charges. So the rate might be advertised as, for example, 7.5%, *typical APR 8.4%*. The APR is the rate to note when comparing 'product prices' between lenders.

Special offers

In the competitive world of mortgage lending, banks and building societies regularly advertise attractive 'special offers'. Some promote incentives such as discounted or reduced interest rates for a set period, whilst others try to attract customers with 'cash back' offers or by agreeing to pay the borrower's legal fees. Often there are one set of deals for those borrowing up to 75% of the purchase price, and another (usually less attractive) for those borrowing 75-95%.

Most of these offers are well worth taking advantage of. The catch is that they tie you to the lender for a period after the incentive runs out. To do this they often stipulate that if you redeem your mortgage within, say 5 years (because you have either sold the property or transferred the mortgage to another lender), you will have to repay the financial inducement, and probably an early redemption charge as well.

• Fixed interest rate

The lenders charge a fixed interest rate for the initial period of the mortgage term. The rate stays the same throughout the fixed-rate period (the length of which varies depending on the current offer) irrespective of general interest-rate fluctuations, so for the first years the mortgage repayments are the same each month. The fixed rate may be slightly higher than the lenders' variable rate, especially if the period is long. Generally, the longer the rate is fixed, the higher the rate will be. You, the borrower, pay more than necessary whilst the lenders' variable rate is below the fixed rate, but you have peace of mind that for the period of the fixed rate the repayments cannot get any higher than they started off. At the end of the reduction period, the rate reverts to the lenders' current variable rate. This type of arrangement can usually be linked to a repayment, endowment, PEP or pension mortgage (see below). A reservation or booking fee is usually charged to secure the funds, and this is currently around £200.

• Discounted interest rate

The lenders discount the rate of interest charged to the borrower for a specified period by a percentage, say 2%, off their variable rate. Generally, the longer the period of discount, the smaller the discount will be. The rate still goes up and down in line with general fluctuations but stays 2% less than the variable rate, whatever that is.

• Cash back/Fees paid

The lenders give you, the borrower, on completion of the purchase, a one-off lump sum of cash which you do not have to repay unless you redeem the mortgage within a specified period. Alternatively, the lenders may agree to pay your legal fees or survey fees, up to a specified amount.

A discounted or fixed interest rate for the initial period of the loan lessens the mortgage burden in the first few months or years. However, do make sure you can comfortably make the repayments when they revert to the lenders' usual variable rate.

What type of mortgage?

It is important to seek expert financial advice when taking out a mortgage. You will, after all, be paying it for many years, so you need to make sure it is the best arrangement for you, now and in the future. This is not something to be entered into lightly, so make sure you fully understand everything about it. If not, ask for clarification. Particularly if you are considering a personal pension plan or a PEP (see below), you must get independent financial advice.

Basically speaking, there are two methods of repaying a mortgage loan and incurred interest. Either you make a single payment to the lenders each month to repay the loan and interest gradually (mostly interest initially, but more of that later), or you make a payment to the lenders to cover the interest only, and take out an investment policy or fund to give enough return to repay the actual loan in full at the end of the term. Hence the two types are referred to as a *repayment mortgage* and an *interest-only mortgage*.

Repayment mortgage

With a repayment mortgage, the loan is repaid gradually over the duration of the term. Initially the monthly payments pay mostly interest, so for the first few years the amount owing on the original loan stays much the same. Gradually the repayments account for more of the loan and less interest until the loan is repaid in full.

45

EXAMPLE: Assuming a £50,000 loan payable over 25 years.

Year	Starting balance	Annual interest paid	Annual capital repaid	Total annual payments
	£	£	£	£
1	50,000.00	3,500.00	790.53	4,290.53
5	46,490.11	3,254.31	1,036.22	4,290.53
10	40,531.09	2,837.18	1,453.35	4,290.53
15	32,173.26	2,252.13	2,038.40	4,290.53
20	20,450.96	1,431.57	2,858.96	4,290.53
25	4,009.84	280.69	4,009.84	4,290.53

Lenders will usually insist on some sort of mortgage protection policy if you do not have sufficient life assurance to pay off the loan in the event of your untimely death. As the outstanding loan decreases over the years, so the insured amount decreases to match the remaining debt, until there is no debt and no cover.

A repayment mortgage is usually cheaper to run than an interest-only mortgage linked to an investment policy (e.g. endowment), but the disadvantage is that there is no lump sum payable at the end of the mortgage and no surrender value.

Interest-only mortgage

If you decide on an interest-only mortgage, you will make two payments each month. One payment covers interest on the loan and one payment covers the premiums on an investment policy taken out to repay the loan. There are several mortgage-linked investment plans:

• Endowment policies

At the end of the mortgage period, the endowment (life assurance) policy should give you an amount which is at least equal to, and sometimes greater than, the amount borrowed so that the loan can be repaid in full.

There is no need to take out extra life assurance since the endowment policy would pay off the mortgage in the event of your death. If you should die before the end of the policy, the life assurance company pays the guaranteed death benefit.

You can usually continue to pay into the endowment policy even if you are no longer funding a purchase, so that you still receive the lump sum on maturity, which is usually tax free. You must, however, advise the assurance company that the lenders no longer have an interest in the policy. The policy can alternatively be surrendered if it is not covering a mortgage, and any accumulated funds withdrawn, or it can be sold to companies or individuals who use such policies as a form of investment.

• Personal pension plans

A personal pension mortgage is similar to an endowment mortgage: You make a monthly payment to the lenders to cover interest on the loan, and a further payment into a personal pension plan. Both payments qualify for tax relief.

You will be required to take out a life assurance policy to cover repayment of the mortgage in the event that you die before retirement. On maturity of the pension policy, i.e. when you reach national retirement age or a chosen retirement date (the end of the mortgage term and the date the policy matures must be the same), the policy provides a lump sum for repayment of the amount borrowed and a pension. The lump sum is tax free, but the pension received from the policy is taxed as earned income at the basic rate after taking account of personal allowances.

This type of mortgage is used as a tax-efficient way of preparing for retirement for those who do not contribute to a company pension scheme. There are, however, restrictions imposed by the Inland Revenue, so financial advice on your individual needs is very important.

DID YOU KNOW? *Lenders do not usually allow the term of the mortgage to run beyond retirement age, so a buyer aged 50 will not be granted a mortgage of more than 15 years.*

• Personal Equity Plans (PEPs)

Similar again to an endowment mortgage, the PEP allows you to build up cash needed to repay the mortgage at the end of the term through investment on the stock market. You would enter into an interest-only mortgage arrangement with the lenders, making monthly payments to cover the interest on the loan, and would probably also need to take out a separate policy for life assurance cover. You then make a second payment into a Personal Equity Plan which invests the funds.

It is possible to vary the amount invested in the PEP, up to a current maximum of £6,000 each year. If the PEP performs well, you may be able to pay off the mortgage early. The amount remaining after the mortgage has been repaid can be taken out as a tax-free lump sum, or you may prefer to continue investing in the PEP. Tax rules have a habit of changing, so whilst a PEP may be tax-efficient now, this might not be the case in the future.

As well as considering which type of mortgage is right for you, think about the length of the mortgage term. If the term is long, then more interest is paid in total, but the monthly repayments are less. If the term is short the reverse applies – high monthly repayments but less interest paid in total.

Mortgage-linked investments are usually intended as long-term arrangements, so if the investment is cashed in or surrendered in the early years, it usually gives the investor a poor return (if any) on his contributions. If you move house, the investment plan can normally be transferred to your next mortgage, but if the loan is increased the plan may need a top-up to make sure it is sufficient in principle to repay the loan at the end of the term.

Beware – investment plans rely on the performance of the investment company and stock markets, so like any investment the value can go down as well as up, giving no absolute guarantee that the plan will generate sufficient funds to pay off the loan. Always seek specialist, independent advice.

The mortgage offer

Once your mortgage application is approved and the property has been inspected by a surveyor, the lenders issue a formal offer of advance, which is, basically, written confirmation of the amount the lenders are willing to lend on a particular property. Once you have this document you can relax in the knowledge that your finance is arranged, assuming of course that the amount is sufficient to fund the purchase.

The offer of advance is usually received a few days after the surveyor submits the valuation report or survey to the lenders, unless there is cause for further investigation, e.g. the surveyor may suggest a detailed report on a specific aspect of the property. The time taken between application and formal offer is usually around two weeks.

Tax

Income tax relief (MIRAS)

If you are buying your home with a mortgage as an owner occupier (i.e. you intend to live in the property), you will be pleased to learn that you are eligible to receive tax relief on the interest you pay, at a rate of 15% at the time of writing. Under the Mortgage Interest Relief At Source scheme (MIRAS for short) the relief is applied to the monthly payments made to the lenders. Because the tax relief is automatically deducted 'at source', you do not need to submit a Tax Return to claim it. Before you start making monthly repayments, you will be asked to complete a form supplied by your lenders, who then send this form to the Inland Revenue. The lenders are then able to calculate the entitled tax relief, reduce the interest charged to you, and claim the shortfall from the Inland Revenue. For you to qualify for MIRAS, the mortgaged property must be your main or only residence.

Only the first £30,000 of the loan is subject to MIRAS, and if the mortgage is taken out jointly between co-purchasers, the tax relief is split between them.

> **DID YOU KNOW?** *The home being purchased could be a houseboat or mobile home and will still qualify for tax relief on the interest paid to purchase it.*

Capital gains tax relief

When an asset such as property is sold for more than the price at which it was purchased, the 'gain' (or profit) is liable to capital gains tax. However, if the property is your main or only residence, you do not have to pay this tax. Only if you were to buy an additional property, perhaps as an investment, would you then be liable to capital gains tax on any profits of the sale, although you can choose which property (the investment property or your own home) you want to qualify for capital gains tax relief, subject to compliance with Inland Revenue rules.

Stamp Duty

Stamp duty becomes due on purchases over £60,000. At the moment it is calculated at 1% of the total purchase price, not just the amount over £60,000. So buyers of a £80,000 property pay stamp duty on the whole £80,000, not just the £20,000 over the threshold.

Costs

Taking out a mortgage, like anything else connected with a property purchase, costs money. It costs nothing to look around for a mortgage, but once the commitment to borrow has been made, the fees start rolling in.

- The lenders may charge a fee to cover administration costs.
- If the mortgage applied for is fixed rate, a reservation fee to reserve the funds at that rate may be charged.
- The lenders usually engage a solicitor to investigate the title (ownership) of the property, and his fee is borne by you. Your own solicitor can act for the lenders in preparing the mortgage.

- A valuation or survey is a mortgage requirement.
- You may elect to take out a Payment Protection Policy (see below).
- The lenders have the right to take out fire insurance on the property, or to insist that you do so. The insurance premium is payable by you, and if this cost is added to the mortgage loan, it will incur interest.
- If you do not take out your buildings insurance through the lenders, they may charge a fee to approve the policy.
- It may be necessary for you to take out life assurance.

If the loan is greater than 75% of the purchase price, an MGI fee may be charged. This is the lenders' indemnity cover which helps them recover the amount owed and any costs if they repossess your home and sell it for less than is needed to clear the debt. It is not insurance for the borrower.

The lenders may charge a fee for sending the amount borrowed to your solicitor so that he can complete the purchase.

These fees and charges relate to the lenders and the mortgage, but there will be others once the purchase gets under way. These conveyance costs etc. all need to be built into the financial picture.

Mortgage repayments

You will be advised of the monthly repayment amount when the mortgage is first taken out, but this figure may go up or down as a result of changes in the interest rate, unless your mortgage rate is fixed, in which case the repayments will remain the same throughout the period of the fixed rate. Payments are made monthly and almost always by direct debit. You will be advised if the monthly repayment amount changes, but you do not usually need to do anything since your bank automatically makes the necessary adjustment to the direct debit.

Repayments are usually deducted from your account at the same point in each month, apart from instances when the date falls on weekends or public holidays. Your lenders will probably have one or two set dates for administration purposes, giving a choice of either the beginning of the month or towards the end, e.g. 6th or 26th.

> **DID YOU KNOW?** *You may be able to reduce your mortgage by making lump sum payments. The number of payments allowed each year is often limited to two, and the amounts may need to be substantial, e.g. in excess of £1,000.*

At the end of the calendar year the lenders will issue a Statement of Account, showing the payments made and a new balance.

Payment protection policies

Your lenders may be keen to recommend that you take out insurance against loss of earnings due to unemployment or ill-health. Such insurance is known variously as Payment Protection, Income Protection etc. and the lenders act as agents for the insurance companies who honour the policies.

But is such insurance really necessary, or is it just another cost home buyers can ill afford? Sadly, the idea that the State will care for its citizens from the cradle to the grave if misfortune renders them incapable of caring for themselves, is simply not realistic, and whilst rented housing is provided through local councils, the State offers little help to those in the process of buying their own property who then become financially embarrassed (see *Mortgage crisis* below).

Payment Protection plans offer some protection, but before you take out this type of policy, it is very important to make sure you are getting the cover you think you are, so read the small print carefully. Make sure you know the following:

- what period of time the policy covers. It is unlikely to be indefinite;
- whether or not the policy pays towards mortgage-related life assurance and investment premiums;
- what the instances of cover are, e.g. redundancy, ill health, unemployment;
- what provision (if any) there is if you are self-employed;
- what the policy does not cover. The list can be very long.

For example if you suffered from an illness less than a year before the policy was taken out and then had a relapse, you probably would not be covered.

A mortgage protection policy should not be confused with life assurance. The latter is not much help if you loose your job or become too sick to work, since it only pays out on maturity or death. The mortgage protection policy, on the other hand, whilst you might pay into it for the entire term of your mortgage, does not pay out a lump sum at the end of the term. A mortgage protection policy is protection against chance, whilst life assurance is more like a form of saving for the inevitable.

Mortgage crisis

'Your home is at risk if you do not keep up the repayments on your mortgage or other loan secured on it.' These words of wisdom appear in one form or other on advertisements for mortgages and on most literature concerning them, warning potential homeowners that they could lose their home if they fall behind with repayments. The statement might make you think twice about your responsibilities when taking on a mortgage, which is a good thing, but since financial difficulties are usually unintentional and unpredictable, as a warning it is pretty useless.

The vast majority of home owners never experience problems repaying a mortgage, so it would be wrong to paint a picture of doom, gloom and financial ruin. But, however remote the possibility, you cannot ignore statistics of (at 1996) over one thousand repossessions every week, so it is sensible to give some consideration to what you would do if you found yourself in a mortgage crisis.

The sad fact is that carefully planned budgets and cautious borrowings, like 'the best laid schemes o' mice an' men', are sometimes not enough to guard against financial crisis. Jobs for life are a thing of the past and redundancy is no longer a rarity in the workplace. Consequently many people become unable to make their monthly mortgage repayments because of reduced circumstances through no fault of their own. This can seem an insurmountable problem if you find yourself in this position, but although there is help at hand if you know where to look for it, it is important to seek help as soon as possible and not wait until the position is desperate.

Possibly one of the worst things to do, likely to push you further and further into debt, is to take out another loan (usually at a higher interest rate and without the benefit of tax relief) to fund mortgage repayments.

If the crisis is temporary, speak to your lenders, some of whom have special telephone help-lines and staff who have been specifically trained to deal with customers in this predicament. What you should not do is let the problem escalate out of hand before seeking help. Sometimes the easiest solution seems to be to walk away from the debt by moving out of the property, but this does not work, and the lenders will take court action against you to recover what you owe. If the lenders sell the property to recover the debt, you will be liable for any costs incurred in so doing, and interest on the loan until the property is sold. If the property sale does not raise sufficient funds to repay the mortgage, you will also be responsible for the shortfall.

> **DID YOU KNOW?** *People who suffer a repossession may be refused a future mortgage if their plight has been recorded on a repossessions register or with a credit reference agency.*

Reputable lenders are usually sympathetic to the predicament of customers who have difficulty keeping up repayments, and most will allow you to make reduced monthly payments in cases of reduced income, or interest-only payments if your income is reduced. They may even, in some circumstances, agree to defer payments for a limited length of time. Ultimately the arrears will have to be recovered one way or another, sometimes by adding them to the outstanding loan, or by an arrangement of supplementary payments. If your reduced circumstances are not temporary, it might be possible to extend the term of the loan to reduce the monthly repayments.

Borrowers who take out a mortgage protection policy may be able to make a claim if they are unable to keep up their monthly repayments, although this type of insurance usually only gives financial help for 12 months. The insurance company must be informed immediately, and before making payments they will need proof of sickness or unemployment in the form of medical certificates (they may also ask for an independent medical opinion) and evidence of claims for unemployment benefit.

State benefits

There are certain state benefits which assist with mortgage repayments, and either the Citizens' Advice Bureau or your local Benefits Agency should be able to give full details of benefit entitlement and how to make a claim.

Who can claim what, when, and how is a minefield of bureaucracy and red tape, so I have attempted to sort through the reams of literature on the subject and identify the relevant points. Briefly then, Job Seeker's Allowance (previously known as Unemployment Benefit), is payable to those people who become unemployed and are actively seeking work. Claimants are expected to sign a contract confirming they are trying to get another job, and if the powers that be feel a claimant is not making enough effort to find work, the benefit could be stopped. In some circumstances, Job Seeker's Allowance includes an amount for payment of mortgage interest.

Income support is a benefit designed to help those on low incomes who work less than 16 hours per week, and also applies to people who have given up work to care for another person, one-parent families, and those who are disabled or too ill to work. Payments may help to pay mortgage interest at the Benefits Agency current standard rate. Income Support may also help with interest payments on loans taken out to make a building fit for occupation, e.g. by the installation of washing and toilet facilities, heating, drainage, ventilation and cooking facilities and for necessary structural repairs. It will not, however, pay back the capital borrowed or endowment policy premiums.

> **DID YOU KNOW?** *If you have savings in excess of £8,000 you will not be eligible for Income Support.*

The amount of Income Support receivable depends on the claimant's income, but basically the standard allowance is calculated and any income is then deducted from that figure. The final figure is the amount you would receive. If you receive income from a mortgage protection policy to pay interest payments not covered by Income Support, these payments will not be counted as income. Similarly, funds received to repay the capital amount of the loan, or to pay premiums on an endowment policy, buildings insurance or the mortgage protection policy itself, will be discounted. A PEP mortgage may be treated as capital for Income Support purposes, so if you have one of these you may not be able to make a claim.

If your loan is high (currently over £100,000), if the property is located in an exclusive area or is much bigger than needed, you might not be eligible for Income Support. Similarly you may become ineligible if your loan was taken out while you were receiving Income Support, if you appear to be renting out space in your home, or if a move from rented property into home ownership has increased your housing costs.

If you fall into arrears, a proportion of your Income Support payment will be paid to your lender towards this debt, but you cannot claim for help with the resulting interest on arrears.

Most eligible claimants have to wait several months after a claim before they receive assistance, so it is essential to apply for the benefit as soon as possible.

The above information is only a guide. It is not conclusive and the system can change, so the Benefits Agency should be approached for full details.

Default and repossession

When you take out a mortgage, your main obligation is to repay the sum borrowed, plus the interest, over the period specified. If you fail to meet this obligation you are in breach of the mortgage contract and the lenders can apply for possession of the premises in order to sell them and recoup the outstanding debt. Thankfully, most lenders are keen to avoid repossession and only take such drastic action as a last resort. They would far rather come to some agreement to allow you to retain your home until the financial crisis has passed.

If the situation gets to a point where you are taken to court by your lenders, you may be able to avoid repossession if you can demonstrate a willingness to make regular payments, albeit less than the usual repayment amount, to the lenders. The payment figure must be realistically within your means, because repossession is only suspended. If you fail to keep up the new payments the lenders can enforce your eviction from the property without going back to court.

Different lenders have different procedures for dealing with customers who cannot keep up repayments, but as a guide the following steps might apply:

• You miss a repayment	Lender writes to bring missed payment to your attention.
• You do nothing and miss two more payments	Lenders write to you to inform you that solicitors are being instructed to apply for a possession order.
• You still do nothing and miss more payments	Lenders apply for a warrant for eviction.
• You are evicted	The property is sold to recover the debt.

The time span from the first missed payment to eviction is usually around a year, but could be as little as 8 months. During this time, interest is being charged on the arrears, increasing the overall debt. If at any time, from the first missed payment to application for an eviction warrant, you sort out a payment schedule to the satisfaction of the lenders, or repays the arrears, the lenders will usually halt eviction proceedings. Even after a property has been repossessed, some lenders will return the keys to the borrower if the arrears are cleared in full.

As the worst scenario, the possibility of repossession cannot be ignored. Recent years have been cruel, and many people have experienced redundancy and greatly reduced circumstances at a time when home ownership is at a peak of popularity. Consequently lenders have been faced with many potential repossession cases, and the problem for both borrower and lender is exacerbated when the property market is in the doldrums. Borrowers in financial difficulty find they cannot dispose of their property quickly before falling so far behind with repayments that repossession is inevitable, and if the property is repossessed, the lender has difficulty selling it to raise enough to clear the debt, leaving the borrower in debt for the outstanding balance.

Negative equity

It is necessary, when looking at mortgages specifically and home-ownership in general, to say a word or two about negative equity – what it is and why it has become so common.

Home-ownership has become very fashionable over recent years. The British public have taken to buying property with great enthusiasm, assuming that whatever their home costs to buy, they will get back with interest when it is sold. However, in the last decade the property market has seen some dramatic ups and downs, so whilst some homeowners made money on property, many lost a great deal.

The lucky ones found that the home they bought rose in value, giving them 'equity' in the property, i.e. the current value less any mortgage or loan. The reverse is the case with negative equity – the homes decreased in value, leaving the owners with a bigger loan than the property is worth. Often negative equity only becomes apparent when the time comes to sell the property, when the value is found to have dropped significantly since it was purchased. Some banks and building societies allow borrowers with negative equity to sell their existing property and transfer the mortgage with negative equity on to a new property. This allows the borrower to move to a cheaper property, so reducing the amount of the mortgage, although the negative equity amount remains the same. The borrower must sell and buy simultaneously because there cannot be a time, however short, when there is no property on which the funding is secured. There are various conditions laid down by lenders in cases of negative equity, so borrowers need to speak to their lenders to see whether or not they comply with these.

It is also possible to move up the property ladder, provided you can afford to take on a bigger mortgage. A 'negative equity mortgage' allows borrowing of up to 125% of the value of the new property. The new arrangement still means you have negative equity – probably more so, as the new loan is 25% more than the property is worth, so if your salary can furnish such a high loan, it would probably make more sense to save the extra spent on increased mortgage repayments, until the negative equity can be cleared from saved funds, rather than borrowing more.

3. BUYING A LEASEHOLD PROPERTY

What is a lease?

Simply put, a lease is a contract granting the right to occupy a property for a specific length of time, usually in return for rent. In the case of buying a leasehold property, the rent is termed 'ground rent'. The person who buys the lease (the *tenant* or *lessee*) temporarily owns the property but not the ground it is built on. Unlike the outright purchase of a freehold property, where the buyer is the absolute owner and can do more or less what he wants with the property, the lessee must comply with any restrictions (or covenants) written into the lease which limit what he can do on, or to, the premises. If you buy a lease, you need to be sure these covenants are reasonable, because if they are not, the lease will be difficult to sell to another buyer in the future.

Generally flats are leasehold and houses are freehold, but there are exceptions. In Scotland leaseholds are a rarity.

Buying a lease is not like renting. Rental tenants and leasehold 'tenants' both enter into an agreement which grants occupation for a specific length of time for an agreed amount of rent, but the apparent similarity ends there. A rental arrangement is usually short term, say six months. Payment for occupation is in the form of a routinely paid rent (weekly or monthly) and this is usually the only payment the landlord receives. Those purchasing a lease, however, enter an arrangement for a much longer period (commonly 100 years) and the lessee pays a one-off payment for the right of occupation (the purchase price), in addition to a nominal 'ground rent'.

Estate agencies' written details should not be relied on to give a full picture of what the buyer of a leasehold property is actually buying. Whereas with a freehold property what you see is mostly what you get, in the case of a leasehold property it is easy to be misled when viewing it. You may, for example, be most impressed with the grounds surrounding the block of flats you view, but be unaware that access to the grounds is not included in the lease. Or perhaps a parking space you use during a viewing does indeed belong to the block, but sadly not to the particular flat you are thinking of buying.

Landlords and lessees

The landlord of a leasehold property owns the freehold, i.e. the block of flats, which he can sell to a third party, who then becomes the new landlord. A new landlord would give notice of a change of ownership so rents would be paid to him. Save for the provisions of the Leasehold Reform Act, a change of landlord should go largely unnoticed by the lessees because the new landlord must operate within the covenants of the leases which have already been granted to the lessees, although the new landlord may be better or worse at fulfilling his obligations and more or less amenable should a problem arise.

The landlord may alternatively dispose of his interest in a block of flats by selling the freehold to the lessees. There may even be a pre-emption arrangement written into the lease, giving the lessees first refusal to purchase the building before it is offered for sale on the open market. Additionally, there exists a statutory right of first refusal, whereby the landlord must give qualifying lessees the opportunity to buy if he intends to sell, and quoting the price.

If you buy a lease, you buy it either from a current lessee or directly from the landlord if there is no current lessee. The lessee can sell (or assign) the period remaining on the lease to you, and you then becomes the landlord's new lessee. All leases run for a specified period of time and naturally the duration left on the lease diminishes as the years pass. If a lease is left to run out of time, the premises eventually revert to the landlord's ownership. Some leases are extended by operation of law on payment of rent.

Some leases contain a clause which gives the lessee the opportunity to renew the lease before it expires. This does not mean that if you own a dwindling lease you can renew it before selling it on, so that it becomes longer and commands a higher selling price. However, if you want to keep the lease you could renew it by giving the required notice before expiry, assuming the terms of the lease contained provision for such a renewal, and the notices are given at the correct time.

If you find yourself with a lease which is not easy to sell because the remaining duration is short, you could always try negotiating an extension with the landlord, but it is usually up to the landlord to decide whether he will grant it or upon what terms. There are exceptions where a landlord can be forced to sell the freehold to the tenant or a group of tenants. It may also be possible for a buyer considering the purchase of a property with a short lease to apply to his potential landlord for an extension, or have a right of renewal inserted in the lease on purchase.

Regardless of whether either landlord or lessee sells his interest in the property to a successor, positive covenants (see below) in the original lease (if prior to 1995) between the first landlord and lessee are binding. In other words, if the freehold is sold and the new landlord fails to comply with a positive covenant, the lessees can seek recompense from the original landlord. Likewise the original lessees continue to have obligations under the covenants they entered into, even if they sell their leases. Since 1995 lessees has been able, in some leases, to relieve themselves of this responsibility.

As a prospective buyer of a leasehold property, you must naturally ensure (or ask your solicitor to ensure) that the person from whom you are buying the lease actually has the right to sell it, and to clarify that the property is free from any third party rights which have not been disclosed. To do this, your solicitor makes a search at the Land Registry to ascertain that the seller's name appears on the register. This is assuming the property falls within the registered system of land transfer, but since most properties in England and Wales do, this is likely to be the case. In the case of unregistered properties, your solicitor will need to examine the title deeds to the freehold and the chain of ownership of the leases.

Restrictions and covenants

Into every lease are written certain restrictions and stipulations which landlord and lessee agree to abide by when entering into the lease agreement. Usually the heavier burden of *restrictions* falls on you as tenant (you must *not* do this or that whilst on the premises), whilst the more onerous *stipulations* apply to the landlord (he *must* repair and maintain the building). Once a restriction or stipulation has been included in a lease, it is generally there for the duration.

Covenants are also included. These are formal promises or undertakings to do or refrain from doing certain things, and let you know what you will be promising if you buy the lease. They usually include payment of rent, and insurance and upkeep of the premises, and may state that the lessee is not permitted to alter the premises, carry on a business there, keep pets etc. Whilst the covenants can seem onerous, they act in a positive way to protect the resale value of the lease by aiming to ensure that the building as a whole does not deteriorate. This is important because the overall appearance of a block of flats reflects on the value and saleability of each of the premises. The landlord promises to allow the tenant 'quiet enjoyment' of the premises and to abide by the stipulations and restrictions imposed on him, e.g. to repair and maintain.

Landlord and tenant have enforceable power over each other to ensure the covenants are complied with, but one tenant does not usually have power over another. Restraining a tenant from committing an act which is in breach of the covenant (perhaps he is causing a nuisance to other tenants) is a matter for the courts by way of an injunction. The court will then order the offender to stop doing whatever it is he is doing which is contrary to the terms of the covenants.

You need to know everything you can about a lease and its covenants, before you consider buying it. The selling agents often have fairly detailed information about the lease as part of their sales details, and initial enquiries concerning specific aspects of the lease can be directed through them. However, the information provided by agents should not be taken as conclusive or complete. Your solicitor is a far better source of factual information since he will be supplied with a copy of the lease by the seller (or his solicitor) from which he can gain specific information, and he will make enquiries on practical matters (services provided and related charges, insurance, boundaries etc.) through the conveyance process.

Anyone considering buying a leasehold property will have specific queries concerning his individual needs and concerns. Since leases are lengthy and complicated documents that use jargon unfamiliar to most of us, it is helpful if your solicitor prepares a summary of the lease in simple language so that you can peruse the key points with ease. You could also ask your solicitor any specific questions. Examples of such questions might include:

- Under what circumstances, if any, does the landlord have the right to enter the premises?
- What repairing obligations, if any, apply to you?
- What repairing obligations apply to the landlord?
- What restrictions are there concerning alterations/improvements to the premises?
- Who insures what, and how is this paid?
- Can business be conducted on the premises?
- How much is the ground rent and service charge; when are they payable and to whom?

In theory, by entering into a lease, both parties willingly agree to abide by the covenants contained in it, and both live happily ever after. But what happens if one or other strays from their agreement and becomes in breach of a covenant? The covenant is only of any use if it is enforceable: if the party who is failing to abide by the covenant can be forced to do so. What could you do if, for example, the landlord is failing in his responsibility to periodically redecorate the exterior of the building?

Firstly, you need to be sure that the landlord really is in breach of a covenant. There is no point complaining that the building is in need of decorating if the landlord is not obliged to carry out the work for another year. If the work is overdue, the first stage of action might be to write to the landlord direct, pointing this out and asking when the work is likely to be put into effect. If this approach does not bring a satisfactory reply and swift action, you may have to take the matter further, through a court order, to force the landlord to stand by his obligations, but the cost, complexities and potential animosity resulting from legal action must make the courts a last resort.

In the case of a landlord's obligation to repair the building, the courts have the power to order the landlord to effect the repairs agreed to in the terms of the lease. Alternatively as a tenant you could arrange for the repairs to be done yourself and then withhold future payments of service charges (if due to the landlord and not a management company) until you have been reimbursed for your outlay. The right to withhold rent is a dangerous one to exercise as a landlord may seek to forfeit the lease for non-payment of rent. If you already have arrears of ground rent, you can write off these arrears against the costs incurred for the repairs. Naturally you must take reasonable measures to ensure the costs are not excessive (by obtaining at least two estimates and employing the contractor who submitted the lower one) and must advise the landlord of your intentions before carrying out the work. You would not have the right, except in an emergency, to enter other flats so it would be trespassing if you went on to such premises without consent to do works, even though the landlord might be in breach of his covenant.

DID YOU KNOW? *In some cases compensation can be sought by landlord or lessee if either party suffers loss as a result of a breach of covenant.*

As well as specific covenants, there are some obligations which landlords are forced to adhere to, whether or not they are mentioned in the lease. These are general rules which are automatically 'implied' when a landlord and lessee enter into their relationship and are an attempt to ensure that the lessee is not subjected to unreasonable or negligent acts by the landlord.

- Regarding the common parts of the building in which a flat is situated and which are 'owned' by the landlord (for example, the stairway), the landlord is obliged to ensure that they are kept in reasonable condition. The landlord is liable to the lessee if he should suffer injury as a result of the area being unsafe because the landlord was in breach of his duty of care.

- The lessee is protected against a negligent landlord who fails to uphold his responsibilities and obligations if such negligence results in damage. Further, the landlord is obliged to ensure that those parts of the building which are in his control are safe for use by the lessees, their visitors and anyone else who might reasonably be expected to use them (the postman, for example). However, generally it is the responsibility of the lessee to ensure that the leased premises are safe, and a person suffering injury in the flat itself (as opposed to the common areas held by the landlord) will direct a complaint or claim for compensation against the holder of the lease.

- Lessees have the basic right to 'quiet enjoyment' of the leased premises, and if the landlord interrupts this quiet enjoyment he is in breach of the implied covenant for this right. 'Quiet enjoyment' is not concerned with problems of noise (which is classed as *nuisance* – see below), but means that the tenant must be free to live in his home without unnecessary interference which could give rise to distress or inconvenience. This could include damage to the lessee's premises as a result of a fault in the building where the landlord has failed to uphold his obligation to repair and maintain. In this case, because of the damage to the flat, the lessee's enjoyment of the premises has been affected. 'Enjoyment' and 'interference' are not to be taken as the effect on a person of unusual sensitivity.

- The lessee has the right to sue the landlord in cases where a breach of the landlord's covenants causes nuisance. This could happen when, for example, the landlord fails in his responsibility to maintain refuse chutes which then become foul smelling and a nuisance to the lessees. Recourse against a landlord who causes nuisance can also be taken up with the Environmental Health Department of the local authority. The Department will investigate anything which is deemed to be a danger to health, and if the landlord is found to be at fault, will specify to him the necessary action to rectify the situation.

The landlord is not, however, normally responsible to each of his lessees for the nuisance actions of any of the other lessees. The landlord may well be willing to act as mediator between lessees in the interests of harmony, and may be an aggrieved lessee's best first approach, but if the landlord is unable or unwilling to resolve a dispute between lessees, there may be no alternative but to apply to the courts for an order against the offender's behaviour, or sue for compensation. (See also Part 2, Chapter 9, *Nuisance*).

Don't forget that a landlord, in dealing with problems or repairs in your block of flats/property does so at your cost, with or without contribution from other tenants. He is seldom placed in the position of having to put his hand in his own pocket.

Service charges

As well as the ground rent, you may have to pay a service charge, usually an annual payment, which will recompense the landlord for his financial outlay in supplying certain services. If you and the other lessees enjoy such services as lifts, these must be maintained, and common areas like entrance halls need to be cleaned and well lit. The cost of services such as these is recouped by the landlord by way of a service charge 'contribution' made by each lessee. Also covered by the service charge might be the general repair and maintenance of the building, insurance, and the landlord's costs in relation to administration and professional fees incurred in the business of overseeing the building.

The potential buyer of a lease needs to ascertain, from the lease, details of the service charge. Not only how much it is likely to be (and they can be very costly), but also exactly what services are covered by the payment and how the charges are distributed among the lessees. In some cases the apportionment of costs may not be equally split, and those whose property is situated on the ground floor, for example, may have a lower service charge than those who would make use of the lift. In some cases, tenants of the larger flats in a block may pay a higher service charge than those in smaller flats, the apportionment being based on floor space or rateable value.

You might not be able to ascertain from the lease exactly how much the service charges will be, which makes budgeting for running costs difficult. You could, however, ask the seller of the lease to provide details of previous service charges to get an idea of what they have been for the last few years.

Usually the lease stipulates a year-end accounting date, at which time the landlord or management company prepares details of annual costs up to that date. The tenants will usually be expected to make estimated payments during the annual period so that the landlord has sufficient funds to pay bills as they arise. At the year end, if the estimated charges have fallen short of the actual costs, you will receive a demand for a further payment to make up the difference. If the estimate was high, resulting in an excess of funds, the excess is usually held against the next year's service charge.

In an attempt to budget for major expenses anticipated in future years, the landlord may set up a 'sinking fund' which enables costs to be spread out and avoids a situation where tenants would need to make a particularly large service charge payment in any one year. If the person you are buying the lease from has an amount held in his name 'on credit' in the sinking fund, you may be asked to reimburse him this amount.

Forfeiture of the lease

If you fail to pay rent (although the amount on a long lease is likely to be minimal), the action open to the landlord is to repossess the premises and effectively cancel the lease. The landlord can only do this if there is a covenant in the lease which stipulates that he may do so in the given circumstances. Non-payment of rent does not automatically end the lease – indeed some ground rents are so small that the landlord does not bother to insist on their payment (although they remain outstanding since it is your obligation as lessee to pay, and not the landlord's obligation to collect), but the landlord has the option of taking severe action if he wishes.

The landlord may also enforce forfeiture if you are in breach of other terms of the lease, but can only do so after you have been given the opportunity to mend your ways and pay compensation if applicable. In other words he cannot intentionally allow you to do something which is contrary to his obligations in order to trap you. The process of the courts in such situations follows a set procedure controlled by particular Acts and timescales, usually giving the tenant ample chance to remedy the problem before it gets out of hand and the lease is terminated. However, the prospect should not be viewed flippantly.

4. BUYING A NEWLY BUILT HOME

Buying a brand-new house or flat has its advantages. You can often gain access before completion, at the builder's discretion, which is very useful when arranging carpet fitting and other preparations before actually moving in. For first time buyers especially, the process of buying a newly built house is considerably less complicated than getting involved in a chain. The deal is just between the buyer and the builder and is not affected by anyone else.

There are problems though, and one of the most obvious is that building work can be subject to delays, leaving the buyer high and dry with no home to move to. This is particularly tricky if you are selling your current home before buying another. You will usually have to vacate your current home by a specific date so that the new owners can move in, but if your new home is not ready by that time you may have to move into temporary accommodation until it is. Because of this potential problem it is worth trying to tie the construction schedule down to a specific date, although this may be difficult.

> **TOP TIP**
> If more than one home is being built on an estate, there may
> be more effort put into finishing those properties which have
> a completion deadline than those which do not.

The newness of a freshly built home is very appealing. It is a clean page, ready to be stamped with your own personality. The decoration is usually acceptable, so there is no need for immediate trips to the DIY store or to spend every foreseeable weekend stripping off old wallpaper. Everything is clean and new. Unfortunately, it doesn't stay that way for long. Pretty soon a brand new home starts to show signs of wear and tear just like any other.

Offers and incentives

As an incentive to attract buyers, builders of new homes come up with all sorts of tempting offers, but buyers would do well to maintain a healthy scepticism when considering these. Rarely do you get something for nothing.

• Cashback

The buyer receives a one-off sum of money from the builder on completion of the purchase. Buyers are attracted to this because it gives them 'extra' cash for the inevitable expenses moving home involves, although they can expect the cash-back sum to be built into the purchase price somewhere.

• Fees paid

The builder agrees to pay some of the buyer's purchasing expenses (commonly legal costs or survey fees), up to a maximum amount. The buyer may have to pay these initially, then apply for a refund. The 'fees paid' incentive is also used by lenders to make their mortgages more attractive to potential borrowers.

• Carpets and curtains

Inclusion of a fitted kitchen and bathroom has become the norm when buying a new home, so it is no longer considered an 'extra'. Nowadays builders have to go one step further and often include new fitted carpets and curtains in the price. Maybe in years to come, new homes will be supplied fully furnished!

• Part exchange

A very helpful arrangement, this one. The builder arranges for the buyer's existing property to be valued, usually by the estate agents who will be employed to sell it, and then makes an offer, probably around 5% below the market value. If the offer is accepted, the double transaction goes ahead and the builder sells the part-exchanged property in due course on the open market. This is a strong incentive for buyers who are having difficulty selling their existing property and for those who cannot face the hassle or time it can take to sell in the normal way.

The first three incentives all involve some sort of financial handout, but in most cases what is given with one hand is taken back with the other, usually in a high purchase price. These offers are particularly appealing to those who have very little ready cash, but have good borrowing status. However, if the purchase price allows for recovery of the incentive, the incentive is effectively being 'bought' along with the property on the mortgage, and thus incurs interest. Sometimes it is better to negotiate a good purchase price instead.

DID YOU KNOW?   *One large national building company has its own 'second hand' outlet, selling those properties it acquired through part exchange deals.*

Visiting a new site

Builders of new houses and flats often install full-time sales staff on site, so it is not always necessary to make an appointment to view the properties, and interested buyers can just turn up. A lot of sites are manned seven days a week, but smaller sites may not be able to afford this luxury, so it is worth telephoning first to make sure someone will be available to show you around. Builders who do not have site offices instruct estate agents to manage sales, so viewings by appointment are arranged through the agency office in the usual way.

TAKE A TIP
Staff employed on site are expert sales people. Buyers should be wary of being manipulated into making a hasty purchase.

The sales office is often located in the garage of the show-house or flat, and here you will find a plan or model showing where each building is to be situated. These plans are useful because you need to look not only at the individual buildings, but at the site as a whole, which can be difficult if construction work is still under way. On sites offering houses of different styles and size, each house type is usually given an identifying name or colour code on the plan, so that even if the site is nowhere near completion, you can see where the building style of your choice will appear in relation to the others. Each style comes with a different price tag, but houses of the same style can also vary in price depending on their site location; one of them, for example, may have a larger garden or a more pleasant outlook.

Beware that site plans and models are not always to scale, and some artistic licence may have been used in preparing them. Because a photograph of the finished site is not possible, the builder's promotional material will probably contain an artist's impression of what the site should look like on completion, but these tend to be rather optimistic and often show more land around or in front of each house than actually turns out to be the case.

When visiting a new site, even if building work is still in progress, you need to view the site as a whole and ask yourself the following:

- Will it be more cramped than the artist's impression indicates?
- Is there sufficient parking?
- Are there any communal green areas, and if so who looks after them?
- Does the arrangement of the site appeal to you?
- How long will it be before all the construction work is completed? You do not want to be living in the middle of a building site indefinitely.
- What is the total number of houses planned for the site?

TOP TIP
Small developments have a habit of growing into large estates. If a development is adjacent to open ground, make sure this land has not been earmarked for a further phase of building.

Then take a look at where your chosen house-type is situated on the site. The position of a property within an estate is vitally important when the time comes to sell it, when the appeal of its newness is past and it becomes just one of many. If it is at the head of the estate, all access traffic will pass your door. The shape of the back garden may mean that a lot of other gardens back on to yours, reducing privacy. If the particular property you like has a good position but is more expensive as a result, you may be able to negotiate with the builders to pull the price into line with the others, especially if your buying position is good. Builders will not want to loose a sale completely for the sake of a small reduction.

A site or estate which already has residents is worthy of a little pre-purchase neighbourliness. The best people to speak to about the benefits and pitfalls of a new estate are those who already live there, so knock on a few doors and ask plenty of questions about whatever is important to you. Ask about the quality of building. If any defects appeared, were they attended to quickly? Did the builder complete the construction according to schedule? Did the new owners get everything they thought they were getting for their money, or were there some omissions on completion? Perhaps they expected the garden to be turfed and the patio laid, but found out later that this was not included in the price. If you know about these things in advance, you may be able to work them into price negotiations. You also get the opportunity to take a close look at your potential neighbours.

Of course not all new houses are built on large sites with many others. Some are built singly, perhaps by a builder employed by the owner of a piece of land, or else are conversions, maybe of a barn; these have become popular in recent years. Whilst large building companies have their reputation to commend them (or not, as the case may be), it is important with a one-off new building or conversion to be sure the builder is of good repute. Bear in mind, also, that whilst a large company will usually rectify a problem with a new house as a matter of normal procedure, an individual builder may prove difficult to tie down to any 'after sale' service.

Having personally seen an individual new house that was built to a design which did not allow sufficient room in the bedroom for a bed, unless it was positioned in such a way that it blocked access to the en-suite bathroom, I recommend you to arm yourself with a tape measure when viewing, to check that the internal specifications work.

Show-houses – staying realistic

Most new house sites prepare show-homes for inspection by potential buyers. At first glance, these show-houses seem to demonstrate how well the building functions as a normal home, with carefully placed items of everyday life giving a 'lived-in' look, as though the owners had just stepped out. However, on closer inspection, everything is a little too carefully arranged to be a true depiction of what the place will look like when someone really does live there.

It is easy to be bowled over by a show-house, but it pays to remember that the property you move into will bear little resemblance to what you see there. The interior designer who decorated the show-house with such care and attention to detail will have passed the job of decorating the other properties to a member of the construction team for little more than a quick coat of emulsion. The furniture will be your own, not specifically chosen to enhance each room, and none of the little touches like co-ordinated soft furnishings, clever lighting etc. will be included in the price.

Try not to be unduly influenced by the aesthetics you see, and bear in mind the tricks of the trade as you browse, such as:

- Lights left on, even in daylight, to make the rooms seem light and airy.
- Smaller-than-average furniture used to make rooms appear larger.
- The salesman will usually invite you to enter each room first, so that he stays out of the line of vision and does not himself crowd the limited space.
- Interior doors may not be hung, because an object as large as a door takes up valuable space. Also, one of the areas where space is often limited is in the hall, so several doors off such a small area would look cluttered.

- Personal effects designed to give the show-home personality are limited to the essentials. You, on the other hand, have all the paraphernalia that comes with normal living.
- Furniture and decoration is usually pale to make rooms look larger.
- Window sizes are exaggerated by carefully arranged curtains.

One of the main drawbacks of a new house is that the rooms are often very small, hence most of the ploys used above are aimed at increasing the illusion of space. It may be an obvious warning to give, but do make sure your furniture will fit, especially in the dining room, an area which is often allotted the smallest space but which needs to take probably the largest piece of furniture you own. Make sure also that you will be able to position your furniture how you like it, not the only way it will fit into the room. Serious design defects are rare, but it is not uncommon to view a show-house and not realise, for example, that the smallest bedroom has room for a bed but for nothing else.

After you have viewed the show-home, you will be given lots of promotional leaflets for you to take away with you, giving information on the type of heating installed, what fixtures and fittings are included, construction details, local amenities and the all-important price list. In most cases the price is negotiable in just the same way as a 'second hand' property, especially if you are in a good buying position and have either exchanged contracts on the sale of your present property or have nothing to sell. The only difference is that negotiations will be direct with the seller, and not indirectly through an estate agent, unless an agency is marketing the site.

Quite often, builders are least open to negotiation in the middle of a building phase. A good advertisement for the site is the number of houses sold, so at the start of building they are keen to sell some quickly to encourage other buyers. Towards the end of the project, there may be some larger houses left unsold, which are sometimes allowed to go for not much more than the next size down, especially if there are only one or two left, and the company is paying sales staff to man the site.

> ### TOP TIP
> The salesperson on site may not have the last word on price negotiations. If he or she refuses a verbal offer, you could try submitting a written one to the regional office (the address will be on the back of the promotional literature). This costs no more than a stamp, but could save a great deal.

If you have not yet sold your current property, the builder may be willing to reserve the home of your choice until you can find a buyer yourself and are in a position to proceed with the purchase. You will usually be expected to pay a deposit, somewhere in the region of £200-£300, to show your commitment. If such an arrangement is entered into, it is important to make sure the builder confirms in writing (to your solicitor's satisfaction) that he will return the reservation fee if he withdraws from the sale, or alternatively that the amount of the reservation fee will be deducted from the purchase price if the sale proceeds. The builder will probably continue to market the property until you can proceed, and if he is approached by some-one else who wants to buy it and can proceed immediately, he will very probably pull out of the deal with you in favour of a quicker sale.

A final reminder if you are buying a new house or flat: it takes a great deal of time and money to turn an empty shell of a building into a home. All the little things which a second-hand house usually comes with (unless the seller is the type who strips the place back to the boards) will need to be bought for a new house. This includes such necessities as curtain tracks, towel rails, bathroom cabinet, light fittings, floor coverings, coat hooks, etc. etc. etc.

The National House-Building Council (NHBC)

The NHBC is a UK organisation which polices its members in the house-building industry. NHBC members have to demonstrate their ability to build to a qualifying standard, and new houses which carry the NHBC Buildmark 10-year warranty have been subjected to visits by inspectors to make sure the buildings comply with construction criteria. This is important because someone who buys a new home only sees it after it has been built, when construction practices which could cause problems in the fabric of the building are no longer visible. Under the Buildmark warranty, buyers are insured against faults which occur as a result of non-compliance with Building Regulations.

The NHBC's Buildmark warranty aims to protect buyers in three ways. Firstly, if you purchase a property still under construction, the NHBC protects against financial loss due to incomplete construction if the builder declares himself bankrupt. Secondly, during the first two years of ownership, the NHBC ensures that builders honour their obligation to rectify faults which are in breach of their standards. Lastly, from the third to the tenth year of ownership, the NHBC itself bears the cost of remedial work to correct major problems caused by structural defects.

> **DID YOU KNOW?** *An extension or conversion may not be covered by the NHBC guarantee, and if the property suffers damage in the course of construction this may not be covered either.*

There is no charge to you for the Buildmark warranty, directly at least, since it is the builder who pays the one-off premium. However, if you make a claim after the second year of ownership, a £100 fee will be charged before the claim can be processed. If your claim is accepted, this fee is refunded. If you make a claim before the second year which goes to arbitration, and the ruling falls against you, you must bear the costs of arbitration. As with any form of insurance, the policy should be read carefully to ascertain exclusions and restrictions.

There can be little doubt that the NHBC warranty is worth having, mainly because construction inspections should prevent defects occurring in the first place. Whether or not your claim is easily or satisfactorily dealt with if a fault does occur would remain to be seen. The warranty should not be relied upon to give ten years free of repairs (wear and tear is not covered), nor should it be seen as reason not to have an in-depth surveyor's report if you have any doubts about the standard of workmanship. The building still needs to be insured – the NHBC will certainly not hold itself responsible for accidental damage, such as a tree falling through the roof or lightning causing the place to burn to the ground.

As an alternative to the NHBC, some builders register with Zurich Municipal, who offer a 'Newbuild Guarantee' (actually insurance) which is similar to the NHBC Buildmark, except that it can be extended to 15 years instead of the more usual 10 years.

Running-in a new house

Problems with the fabric of a new building are no more likely than with that of a 'second hand' property, but a new house does require a period of running-in, mainly because of the number one enemy of any building – water. During construction, the building will have absorbed water – lots of it. Most of the materials – wood, brick, plaster etc. – are porous, so the building starts off damp and needs to be dried out gently. As this drying-out occurs, the wood and plaster often shrink and begin to show tiny cracks. At the same time, the moisture released into the air causes condensation.

These problems are unavoidable, but can be kept to a minimum by heating the property gently and evenly, and helping air to circulate by leaving windows and internal doors open as much as possible. Most of the condensation caused by the damp building materials eases once the property has been occupied. Any which persists on windows should always be wiped away as soon as it appears, to avoid permanent damage to the frame.

Resist the temptation to redecorate your new home until it has properly dried out. This could take around six months, but ask the builder's advice.

Precautions

It is difficult to imagine anyone buying something as intricate and expensive as a property without seeing it completed to their satisfaction, or fully built at least. But sometimes, especially when a development is small and the properties in demand, you may be faced with a choice of either making a commitment to buy at the early stages of construction, or missing out on the purchase altogether. In this predicament, you should quite rightly be concerned that the build-quality of your new home comes up to scratch. After all, you must ask yourself whether the builder will be as diligent in his work once the sale has been agreed and he has no further need to impress. Possibly not, so potential buyers need to protect themselves as best they can.

- Find out whether the builder is on the NHBC's register. If not, why not?
- Check the history of the site. Is it a reclaimed landfill or ex-industrial site? If so, there could be future complications from soil pollution and stability problems. 'Brown field' sites need extra investigation.
- Make sure you know what to expect from the standard of finish. Will the garden be turfed? Will the loft be boarded? Will the bathroom be fully or part tiled? etc.
- Get written confirmation of extras, e.g. choice of fitted kitchen, bathroom etc.
- If possible, tie the builder down to a specific completion date, allowing sufficient leeway for inevitable delays.
- Make sure a reservation deposit is returnable if the purchase does not conclude for any reason.
- Make sure you know what restrictions there are (for example, you may not be allowed to fence the front garden area) and satisfy yourself that you are happy to comply with them.

A final point

It is often not the style or location of a new home that sells it, but the mere fact that it is brand new. Should you ever come to sell your new home, you will have to compete for a buyer with dozens, perhaps hundreds, of similar modern houses, especially if the property is on a large estate. What is more, rather like a new car which depreciates in value the moment it is driven off the garage forecourt, your new home could value once it becomes second hand.

5. BUYING AT AUCTION

The amount of property bought and sold at auction accounts for only a tiny percentage of general property transactions, mainly because the auction system is an unknown quantity. For most people, making an offer direct to the seller (the *private treaty* system) seems far easier and less daunting than making a bid at auction, because buying at auction is instant. Once a bid is accepted and the hammer falls, the commitment to buy is binding, whereas making an offer through the normal channels gives the buyer time to back out of the purchase if he changes his mind (although remember that the system in Scotland differs from that in the rest of the UK).

> **DID YOU KNOW?** *If a successful bidder retracts from the purchase by absconding from the auction without signing the contract of sale, the auctioneer may sign the contract on his behalf and the sale is still binding.*

Some people reject buying at auction because they do not know how the process works. They imagine that bidding might happen so quickly that the property they want to buy could be sold to someone else before they have a chance to bid. Some even worry that a sneeze or scratch of the head at a crucial moment might result in a bid inadvertently being made. In reality it is very unlikely that a slight body movement would be misconstrued by an auctioneer, who is expert at recognizing what is a bid and what is not. Unless you scratch your head whilst making direct eye contact with the auctioneer, perhaps nodding at him and winking at the same time, the auctioneer will recognise a scratch for what it is.

Another reason why auction rooms do not attract more buyers is that people assume they need ready cash to buy at auction, when in fact in many cases it is perfectly possible to obtain a mortgage in the usual way.

It is essential to plan ahead to arrange funding in advance (as well as some of the conveyancing work and a survey or valuation), but it is not impossible. Unfortunately, having done all this advance preparation, if your bid is unsuccessful any costs incurred are wasted.

What type of property is sold at auction?

Buyers often imagine that the only type of property sold at auction will be large country estates or, at the other end of the scale, mortgage repossessions. Not so. Because many people who buy at auction nowadays are owner-occupiers, and not builders and property speculators as used to be the case, there is a huge variety in the type of property sold at auction. The number of properties offered at any one auction varies from one event to another. Multiple auctions tend to be for disposal of repossessions, whereas auctions of private homes usually deal with just one or two properties at a time.

Almost any property can be sold at auction, but some traditionally sell more successfully than others, particularly those which are:

- Worth less than £100,000
- Older style (pre 1900)
- In need of modernization and/or improvement
- Situated in an attractive location.

Properties like this generally attract a good attendance of potential buyers, and the competition pushes the price up, so if this is the type of property you are looking for, you probably won't be the only one interested.

It is a mistake to assume that a property sold at auction will be any cheaper than if it were sold in the usual way, so don't assume that you will get a bargain. Know in advance what the property you are interested in is worth, and stick to your budget.

Properties 'in need of modernization' receive a lot of interest, especially if the guide price (see below) is tempting, because they seem like a good buy compared to similar properties in fair condition. A word of warning. Buying such a property can be a false economy. You may think you have found a bargain, but more often than not the modernization work will be a good deal more expensive than anticipated. Buyers with a good imagination see a basically sound building which simply needs tidying up – a new kitchen and bathroom, maybe an internal wall knocked down, a window or two replaced, central heating installed and some general redecorating. No problem, they think. A few thousand pounds should be enough, and most of the work can be done by a DIY enthusiast without the expense of employing professionals. If this sounds like you, prepare to face a money pit, and working every weekend for the foreseeable future.

Renovating a property can be both rewarding and profitable, if you know what you are doing, but it is very hard work to do most of the labour yourself. If you choose alternatively to employ a team of builders and craftsmen, the expense of this, plus the initial purchase price, can far outweigh the value of the finished property, so it is imperative to know *before* the auction exactly how much the improvements will cost before deciding how much it is worth bidding. Living in a property whilst improvements are being carried out can be a nightmare. The persistent dust and upheaval quickly becomes trying, and the work usually goes on for much longer than expected. Of course it is all worth it to get the home of your dreams, or a bargain, but you could find after all your hard work that you could have bought, for less than the final cost, a similar property which someone else had slaved over.

If you buy a property in need of modernization, you will probably only be able to borrow enough to buy the property itself, and may need to take out a bridging loan to pay for improvements if you do not have the cash yourself. This is also the case when buying a plot of land to build on. A mortgage can be secured on the land itself, but not on the new building until it is completed.

Preparing for an auction

Not all estate agencies handle auctions. Most who do are Chartered Surveyors by profession, so the Royal Institute of Chartered Surveyors is the body to approach for a list of those who operate in the area, or you could look in the local telephone directory for advertisements listed under 'Auctions'. Armed with this information, you can register with the relevant agents, and will in due course receive details of properties to be auctioned. If any of them are of interest, arrange for an appointment to view through the selling agent in the usual way.

Once you find a property worth bidding for, you will need to start arranging some of the paperwork in advance of the auction date.

- If you need a mortgage, this must be arranged in advance so that funding is in place on the day of the auction, although obviously you do not know beforehand exactly how high you will need to bid to secure the property. You may be pleasantly surprised, or you may lose the property to a higher bidder. Lenders do not normally concern themselves with the amount you actually pay for the property, but they will specify in your mortgage offer the maximum they are prepared to lend. If you decide to bid higher than the lenders' valuation, that is entirely up to you, so long as you can meet the amount above the mortgage from your own funds. If the property is acquired for less than the valuation, it may cause difficulties if the mortgage arranged is a percentage of the valuation. Your lenders can usually amend their offer to reflect this without much delay, but you will need to contact them as soon as possible to arrange this.

- Before issuing a mortgage offer, the lenders will want a valuation report or survey carried out to ascertain the property's value and condition. The lenders will probably arrange this in the usual way. A full survey is no more necessary for an auction purchase than for a conventional purchase, although if the property is in a state of disrepair, the lenders may insist on a detailed report, and may impose a retention (i.e. withhold part of the loan) until repairs are completed.

- Certain aspects of the conveyance need to be carried out in advance of the auction to ensure that the purchase goes smoothly and to protect you, but the paperwork involved is much the same as a for normal purchase. Your solicitor will need to obtain the same information, complete the same forms and attend to the same details as for any conveyance, but the sequence is slightly different. For an auction sale, the contract is ready for signature on the day of the auction (prepared by the seller's solicitor). In order for you to be in a position to sign the contract, your solicitor should approve it before the auction. The exchange of contracts happens on the day, and legally binds you to complete the purchase. The seller's solicitor will usually have obtained the normal searches through the local authority, which will be available for inspection, and your solicitor needs to make sure the property has a sound title before you buy it.

• A deposit, commonly 10% of the purchase price, is paid by the buyer on signature of the contract, so sufficient funds need to be made available to pay this on the day of the auction. The auction particulars may specify whether a personal cheque is acceptable, or whether some form of registration and proof of financial probity is required.

All of the above are necessary administrative preparations prior to an auction, but even more importantly, you must prepare yourself. Before attending the auction, you should know exactly what the property is worth, and should not be tempted to bid above this figure. This maximum may not necessarily be the most you can afford, but it is as much as the property is worth to you. If you know yourself well enough to suspect that having a sensible maximum in mind might not be enough to halt the temptation to bid higher, you could try setting yourself two figures. The first is as much as the property is worth, the second is a *slightly* higher figure which is more than it is worth. You enter the bidding knowing this last figure is right on the edge of reason, and to bid any higher would be madness. Decide on a system which is best for you, but never attend an auction with the intention of 'going with the flow'.

At the end of the day, you must accept that you will lose out one way or another if someone else is interested in the same property and is willing to bid higher. Either you will fail to secure the purchase, or else you will pay more than it is worth. The latter is, of course, to be avoided, but it is all too easy to let emotions get out of hand when you can see your rival sitting a few feet away. It is virtually impossible not to dislike this person who is trying to out-bid you, and as the bidding progresses, sense and reason often fail in the face of inexperience and a determination not to be beaten.

The picture is a common one. You start bidding tentatively, then gains confidence as other buyers drop out. The bidding edges towards your maximum, but now it's a two-horse race. The remaining competitor looks comfortable, so you wonder if he could be an investor. If so, reason suggests he has to make a profit, so you know he cannot afford to pay over the odds. You make your maximum bid confidently, but the investor raises his hand again. Perhaps he knows something you don't. The auctioneer looks to you to raise the stakes with another bid. You make just one more. The property, previously desirable, is by now absolutely essential to you. The competition makes another bid, taking the price past your maximum but still affordable, so you raise your hand again. A pause, then the auctioneer takes another bid from the opposition. You fume inwardly, but bid again, confident of success because you know the property isn't worth any more. Another bid from the other side of the room, but tentatively this time. One more bid should do it. Just to be bloody minded, the competitor raises the stakes once more. Well two can play at that game. SUCCESS. The competitor shakes his head and you are the proud owner. But at what price?

TOP TIP
Familiarize yourself with the system by attending one or two
auctions before you start bidding.

Attending an auction

A few days before the auction date, you should confirm with your solicitor that all the necessary paperwork is in place – the searches have been received and are in order, the Preliminary Information Form has been completed, and the contract approved. You will by this time have arranged mortgage funding and the survey or valuation will have been carried out to both your and your lenders' satisfaction. All that remains is to secure the purchase on the day.

DID YOU KNOW? *Auctions are not always held in auction rooms. Quite often the village hall or local pub is used, or indeed the property itself.*

There is no need to arrive at the auction venue particularly early, but do allow sufficient travelling time to avoid arriving late or having to hurry. There could be several properties being auctioned, giving you an opportunity to watch other sales before the auctioneer starts the bidding on the one you are interested in. If the bidding is slow to start, the auctioneer can make bids himself up to the reserve price. This is common practice, but not usually noticeable to the untrained eye, so you might assume quite wrongly that other people are making bids. The auctioneer is not acting illegally – the seller, via the auctioneer, commonly holds the right to bid to the reserve price.

The way to make a bid is simply to attract the auctioneer's attention by, for example, raising your hand. Once the auctioneer sees that you are bidding, he will look towards you periodically to see if you wish to increase your bid. If you are in competition with more than one other buyer, you may choose to let them battle it out between themselves and wait until all bids have been received before entering the ring, assuming the price is still within your limit. Care needs to be taken with this strategy, since you need to make your bid before the hammer finally falls or else lose the property.

The auctioneer cannot make you bid against yourself. In other words, if you make a bid above the reserve price and nobody answers the auctioneer's next price call, he cannot look to you to better your last bid, so the property becomes yours. If you cannot see anyone else bidding but the price keeps rising, you know somebody is in competition with you.

> **DID YOU KNOW?**   *Your solicitor can attend the auction to bid on your behalf. He will require signed instructions prior to the auction, and needs to be in possession of cleared funds sufficient for the deposit.*

If your bid is successful, i.e. the highest, you will be expected to sign the contract and pay the deposit there and then. Details of your solicitor are routinely requested, although often in practice your solicitor and the solicitors acting for the seller have liaised already concerning the contract.

It is worth stressing that if your bid is successful you are legally bound to complete the purchase.

Pricing

Many people assume that a property being sold at auction will fetch less than it would if sold by an estate agent, which is not necessarily the case. It is true to say that some sellers are determined to sell at almost any price to dispose of a property, but not many are, and if competition for a particular property is strong it could fetch *more* than the market price. Do not therefore assume that buying at auction is the way to find a bargain, and be prepared to let a property go if competitive bidding pushes the price beyond its real worth.

• Guide Price

The Guide Price is the advertised price and is often lower than the seller expects to achieve. The figure is pitched to attract as much interest as possible, so that on the day of the auction there are plenty of eager bidders in competition with each other. It is unrealistic for a buyer to assume that you will secure a property for the amount of the Guide Price, which is not necessarily an indication of the reserve price (see below).

• Reserve Price

This is the lowest price the seller is willing to sell for, and the auctioneer will not accept a final bid which is lower than this amount. The existence of a reserve price will be mentioned in the auctioneer's Conditions of Sale although the actual figure remains confidential. If no-one bids above the reserve price, the property will remain unsold. The auctioneer does not necessarily start the bidding at the reserve price, since he wants to encourage plenty of lively bidding to start proceedings.

Insurance

If your bid is successful, once the hammer falls you should have buildings insurance in place, since you now have a 10% interest in the property and are committed to buy it even if it burns down between the auction and the date of completion. The seller will probably have insurance, but this cannot be relied upon.

Costs

The costs involved in purchasing at auction are much the same as purchasing on the open market, although since your solicitor will need to carry out much of the conveyance prior to the auction, you may be asked for part payment in advance to cover the cost of search fees etc.

If you are not successful at the auction, you will still incur, or have incurred, costs. Your solicitor will require payment for the work he has done, arrangement fees may have been charged by your lenders if a mortgage has been arranged, and the valuation or survey will already have been paid for.

If you buy at auction with your own funds, you can avoid wasting money on unsuccessful bids because you do not have mortgage fees and do not *have* to obtain a survey as long as you are confident and competent enough to buy without one. Furthermore, cash buyers might only employ a solicitor if their bid is successful, although they run the risk of acquiring a property with a dubious title or local land charges if these are not checked beforehand.

Completion

Since much of the conveyance work is done in advance of the auction, and there is no chain involved, completion can be achieved quickly. Usually this takes place around 28 days after the auction, but in theory it could be as soon as the following day if both you and the seller wish it, and if their solicitors have completed the paperwork. The conveyance procedure post-exchange of contracts is much the same as for private treaty purchases. If the property being bought carries an existing mortgage, the seller's solicitor arranges for this to be redeemed, and if you are using a mortgage this will be effected in the usual way.

The date for completion is included in the contract, so since you solicitor will already have had sight of the contract, you will know what this date is before the auction. Completion takes place in the usual way, when solicitors acting for both parties oversee the transfer of documents and delivery of purchase funds. The key is then made available so that you can take possession.

Offers prior to auction

If you wish, you can sometimes approach the selling agents and make an offer for a property before it goes to auction. If your offer is accepted, the property is then withdrawn from the auction, but only if the contract of sale is signed before the date of the intended auction. If not, the seller may allow the auction to continue because his concern is that you could back out of the purchase, leaving him high and dry. If the seller refuses your offer and the auction goes ahead but the property fails to reach its reserve price, the seller might then reconsider and accept your offer. Since it is then obvious that the auction failed, this could put you in a strong negotiating position.

Occasionally, the selling agents may instigate an unofficial telephone auction. If, for example, the agents receive an offer prior to auction from Mr First, they may then telephone Mrs Second, who has also shown an interest in the property. The agent explains that the seller is considering an offer received prior to auction (although he should not disclose the amount), and asks if Mrs Second would also like to make an offer.

Mrs Second might refuse, or she might make an offer which she hopes is higher than Mr First's. If it is, the agent then goes back to Mr First with the bad news that a higher offer has been received, in response to which Mr First might increase his own offer. If so, the agent returns to Mrs Second to see if she will better her offer, and so on until both potential buyers have their cards on the table and the highest offer is reached. Understandably, this system is not popular with buyers, and the property may still go to auction if the final offer is not high enough.

Sometimes, when an agent is marketing a property for auction but a disappointing response makes him doubt it will reach its reserve, he may use another method to prompt a sale prior to the auction by inviting written offers to be received by a particular date. Because potential buyers do not know what other potential buyers will offer, or even if there are any, the agents hope that the interested buyers will submit their very best offers or risk losing out to a higher bidder. When the offers are received, the seller has the option of accepting the best one, or taking his chances at auction. A good offer will only be accepted if the buyer is able to meet a deadline of, say, 14 days to sign a contract of sale. If he is not able to meet this deadline, the property will usually still go to auction, or alternatively the next best offer may be accepted in the same way if there is sufficient time. From the seller's point of view, there are advantages because he has saved some of his auction expenses and may well attract more offers in this way than he could expect to receive from buyers who might be unable or unwilling to bid at auction. Potential buyers often find this arrangement preferable to bidding at auction because they do not have any expenses if their bid is not accepted.

This type of 'best bids' system is, for buyers, fairer than the telephone auction, but for the seller the telephone auction often unearths a higher offer. In either situation buyers would be unwise to offer more for a property than they would if it had gone to auction. Both systems force buyers to bid in the dark, in that they do not know the amount of other offers and, with telephone auctions, they only have the agent's word for it that there have been any. Agents usually reserve the right to reject offers, even the best ones, if they consider they are not good enough.

Advantages and disadvantages

The main advantage of auctions to both buyer and seller is that they can save time and circumvent a lot of uncertainty. Because the purchase is secured on the day, there is no chain involved and the period between the auction and completion is usually only about a month or less. The seller has the advantage of knowing that the property will almost certainly be sold on the day, assuming the reserve price is low enough.

The disadvantages mainly affect potential buyers. You can go to a lot of trouble to prepare for an auction and then be out-bid by the competition, losing the property and incurring costs. Also, there is no 'cooling off' period between making an offer and exchange of contracts, during which you could back out of the purchase if it was a mistake. And lastly, if you are not careful, you could end up paying more for a property than its market value. Aside from the temptation to out-bid the competition, this can also happen because property sold at auction is often unique, so without knowledge of comparable properties it is difficult to estimate a true value.

6. CONVEYANCING

The term 'homeowner' is often used as a convenient description of a person who sets out to own his home, but literally speaking the correct term should be 'land owner'. In legal terms the permanent building on a piece of land is secondary to, and forms part of, the purchase of the land itself. Documents relating to a purchase (a transfer from one person to another) use terms like 'purchase of the land together with the dwelling house known as (the address)', or for new buildings 'all that plot of land situated at . . . and intended to be known as (the address)'.

So is a property (or land) ever really owned? If it is purchased using a mortgage or other form of secured lending, the mortgagee (the lender) holds the deeds, as security until the loan is repaid in full. The 'homeowner', therefore, only has an interest in the property. The homeowner has more rights over the property than the lender (he can rent it out, sell it, occupy it etc.) but he does not 'own' the property outright until such time as there are no loans secured on it. Even when financially speaking the homeowner is the sole holder, he must accept and comply with certain restrictions on the use of a property (or land). For example, he can only use it for permitted use under the Planning Acts and cannot erect structures which do not have planning permission. Representatives of authority (such as the police and customs officers) can enter the property under certain circumstances in the course of their duty, so the property is still not the homeowner's sacred domain.

> **DID YOU KNOW?** *The homeowner owns the soils under his property and the air directly above it, but he does not own any water which flows over it by river.*

Buying a property (or more accurately the land) – the process of transferring ownership from the present owner to you – involves some unavoidable paperwork. Documents have to be drawn up for signature by both you and the seller, information must be obtained and conditions declared. The process can be lengthy, not because it is particularly complex but because it relies on a lot of people to supply information. The seller needs to supply information about the property (guarantees etc.), you have to supply information about your funding, your lenders need information on the property, information is requested from the land registry etc. etc. The orchestrators and collectors of this veritable mountain of paper, who have their fingers on the pulse of the proceedings, are the solicitors acting for you and the seller.

> **DID YOU KNOW?** *One solicitor cannot generally act for both buyer and seller. Such an arrangement could lead to a conflict of interests.*

Choosing a solicitor

NOTE: Nowadays, solicitors do not have a monopoly on the job of conveyancing, and you can alternatively use licensed conveyancers (in Scotland, qualified conveyancers) who are not necessarily solicitors but act as a parallel profession specializing in the legal transfer of property. For purposes of simplicity, however, the term 'solicitor' has been used in this book to refer to a legal representative and encompasses licensed conveyancers as well as solicitors.

You can obtain some names of local conveyancers and solicitors by contacting the following:

- In England & Wales – The Society of Licensed Conveyancers (Tel: 0181 681 1001) or the Law Society (Tel: 0171 242 1222)
- In Scotland – The Scottish Conveyancing and Executry Services Board (Tel: 0131 226 7411) .

If you presently use a firm of solicitors for other legal matters and are happy with their services, or if you still have the name of the firm you used when purchasing a property in the past, you may as well instruct them to handle the conveyance. One solicitor handles a conveyance in much the same way as another, and whilst the technical competence of solicitors does come into question occasionally (which is one of the reasons you should use your own initiative and not rely exclusively on your solicitor), with professional experience most of them can handle a conveyance standing on their head, blindfold, with both hands tied behind their back.

If you intend asking your chosen solicitor to deal with matters in addition to the conveyance (perhaps you are moving because of divorce) it may be helpful and less complicated if one solicitor deals with everything. In this instance a licensed conveyancer (who is only able to deal with conveyancing matters) would not be a suitable choice, and you need to check that the solicitor you choose is willing and able to handle matters other than conveyancing, since they often specialise in one area of legal work only. If your solicitor only does conveyance work, one of his colleagues in the same firm may be able to act for you in other matters, cutting down on postage delays between solicitors and hopefully aiding liaison.

TAKE A TIP

During the course of their lending business, banks and building societies deal with solicitors all the time, so you could ask your lenders to recommend any firms who have proved themselves efficient in past dealings.

You do not necessarily need to use a firm of solicitors who are local to you, which is just as well if buying and selling in different parts of the country, when it is advantageous for one solicitor to handle both transactions to reduce the flow of correspondence. Generally speaking the fewer people involved, the less chance there is of delays. Years ago, it was useful to use a local firm because the solicitor handling a conveyance would physically visit the property his client was purchasing, in order to obtain first hand knowledge about the location etc. This is rare nowadays, and since most information handled by a solicitor is sent through the post (document exchanges) or by fax, or is dealt with over the telephone, it doesn't really matter if you are buying a home in Liverpool and your solicitor has never been north of Watford.

Fees

If you turn to the telephone directory to make your choice of solicitor, be sure to speak to at least three different firms to get an idea of the fees they charge. They can vary enormously. Charges are usually based on the value of the property, so when you ask for a quote, the solicitor will want to know what the purchase price is. The charge a solicitor makes for his time and attention is much the same for a purchase as it is for a sale, but the many other costs involved in a purchase, e.g. search fees and land registry charges, make buying a property more expensive than selling one.

Agree the fee with your chosen solicitor before instructing him to start work on your behalf. If you do this over the telephone, follow up the conversation with a short letter setting down details of the property (the address, purchase price, name of seller, selling agents), your own details (name, present address, telephone number) and the quoted fee. It is useful at this stage to ask the solicitor to clarify any other costs you can expect to incur, which will help you to budget. You will probably receive a quote like this, which assumes a simultaneous purchase and sale:

BRADLEY & CO. SOLICITORS

Mr & Mrs Buyer
The Nook
13 Stock Lane
Westongate
Avon

Dear Mr & Mrs Buyer

Re: Purchase of 22 Bishops Avenue
     Sale of The Nook

I write to confirm my quotation in connection with your above sale and purchase as follows:

	£	£
Legal fees in connection with purchase @	54,000	295.00
Legal fees in connection with sale @	50,000	295.00
		590.00
VAT @ 17.5%		103.25
Local Search Fees		56.00
Office copy entries		14.00
Land Registry fees		140.00
Other searches (estimate)		5.00
Telegraphic transfer fee		30.00
Total		938.25

I trust this is satisfactory.

Yours sincerely

Some solicitors offer 'cut-price' conveyancing, but this could become a thing of the past in England and Wales if the Governing Council of the Law Society concludes plans discussed in December 1995 to force solicitors to increase the fees they charge. The reason for such a move follows concern that some solicitors are cutting corners in order to offer a cheaper service. Competition in the profession is such that conveyancing fees have been forced down to a level at which solicitors can no longer afford to spend sufficient time and attention on each case. The cut-price quote may cover the cost of a straightforward purchase, but problems arise when complications demand more time than the solicitor's quote can possibly cover, resulting in claims of inadequate attention to important details.

Wide consultation in the profession will decide whether to set quality standards in return for compulsory minimum fees in an effort to stamp out cut-price conveyancing, and if this goes ahead consumers can expect conveyancing fees to rise. There are also moves afoot to have separate representation for the buyer and his lenders, which could add to purchase costs.

Working together

The way to get the best out of your solicitor is to work with him. If he asks you to obtain a particular piece of information or to sign something in the presence of a witness, do it promptly and do it properly. Any instructions received should be carefully read and dealt with efficiently.

In most cases, the purchase of a property follows the simple process of the seller supplying various items of information to, and then swapping certain documents with, the buyer (although in practice each acts through his solicitor). This process is not complicated but is subject to delays, mainly because of the sheer number of people involved. Postal delays are also a problem. When you consider that a document may need to go from the seller to his solicitor, from there to your solicitor, then to you and possibly to the mortgage lenders and their solicitor, then back again, it is easy to see how a single document can take a fortnight to be dealt with. If there are a lot of documents winging their way through the postal system, this adds up to a lot of fortnights. Postal delays aside, the buyer is able to speed up his side of the proceedings by using a little forethought.

- Mortgage funding can take time to arrange, so speak with the mortgage officer at your bank or building society as soon as you know you will be moving, and do not delay in supplying them with the information they request. Many lenders agree lending in principle, provided the property when found comes up to valuation. If you are selling your current home as well as buying, give your solicitor your current mortgage account number and details.
- If you have a specific query, perhaps regarding clarification of a boundary, raise this early on. Your solicitor may be unaware of the problem and will need to apply for information from the seller, through the land registry or similar, and it could take time for this information to be supplied back to him.

Not all delays can be circumvented, but when you consider that the largest proportion of conveyancing is concerned with trying to obtain information and agree dates, you begin to see how thinking ahead can help speed up the process.

As mentioned earlier, solicitors rarely visit a property being purchased, so they do not have the opportunity to anticipate problems through personal observation. It is therefore up to you to supply your solicitor with any relevant information about the property which may not be immediately apparent, for example a right of way over the garden. The selling agent's details give your solicitor some valuable information, so this is one of the pieces of information you should make sure he has to hand before the purchase gets under way. For example, the written details may give directions on how to find the property, mentioning that 'access is obtained down a private road'. You may not see this as a problem, and it may not be one, but the solicitor needs to clarify whether or not the road is 'private' only in a graphic description of its seclusion, or whether it really is private property. If so, clarification will be needed on what rights you would have over the road, and who is responsible for repair and maintenance.

The seller will need to supply various documents. If his solicitor acting for the seller is on the ball, he will ask for these documents early on in the proceedings, otherwise the seller will find himself desperately hunting for elusive bits of paper which are, by that time, urgently needed. The seller may need to contact his landlord (if the property is leasehold) or need insurance documents, all of which takes time, so you could ask your solicitor to prompt such action. Some of the information your solicitor needs before the purchase goes ahead will include:

- Copies of service charges and ground rent charges for the last three years (for leasehold properties) with the latest receipts.
- In Scotland, details of factor's charges or similar.
- The builder's NHBC guarantee or equivalent if the property is still under guarantee (under 10 years old) or under construction.
- Documents relating to building alterations (planning permission/ building regulation documents/building control warrants).
- Guarantees for repairs like damp-proofing or wood treatment.
- Details of buildings insurance.

If there is anything about the purchase that you are unsure of, or would like clarification on, don't wait for your solicitor to raise the issue – ask him yourself. That is what you are paying him for.

When approaching lenders for funding, they will ask for details of your solicitor. Most lenders do not process a mortgage application without these details, so you are well advised to choose your legal representative before approaching lenders to avoid unnecessary delays.

TOP TIP

Clarify the name of the particular solicitor who will be handling your conveyance and always ask to speak to him or her personally when telephoning. Do not accept being dealt with by whoever happens to answer the call – they are not aware of your case or any particular concerns you may have.

DIY conveyancing

If you have common sense, are determined to save money and have the temerity to question whether conveyancing can *only* be done by a solicitor or conveyancer, you may decide to do your own. Personally I have yet to deal with a solicitor who did not do an excellent job, and would not have the time, energy or inclination to take on the job of conveyancing myself, but you may feel differently.

For most people, the belief that solicitors are infallible is reason enough for enlisting their services, and most of us choose to relax in the knowledge that the conveyance is being dealt with by someone who knows the system. However, solicitors can make mistakes and, more important, they are perhaps not as diligent as an interested party. This diligence is especially important when buying a property, since relevant issues such as proposed buildings or new roads are only uncovered by direct contact with the local authority. If you use a solicitor you might assume that his diligence and mysterious 'searches' are bound to uncover every issue relating to the property, so do not bother to find out for yourself, when if fact there may be some things which require further investigation or clarification which the solicitor does not report on.

Common practice implies that you need a solicitor for conveyancing in much the same way as you need a dentist remove a tooth. However, there is no law that says you can't remove your own teeth, and similarly you are quite at liberty to handle the considerably less painful task of administering a property purchase (or sale, for that matter).

However, if you have no experience of dealing with authority, if you are not able to express yourself concisely, if you are daunted by officialdom, if you want to complete the purchase quickly, if you do not have plenty of spare time, if you are not prepared to read widely on the subject, and lastly, if you hate paperwork, don't even consider it.

TOP TIP
If buying and selling simultaneously, you don't have to do
your own conveyancing on both transactions.

There are many potential pitfalls in a DIY conveyance, especially where a property is being purchased. The only real advantage (apart from being able to say you did it) is financial, but given that your lenders will almost certainly instruct their own solicitor if the borrower is not employing one, and there are no prizes for guessing who will have to pay the fee, the savings could end up being hardly worth the bother.

If you are selling as well as buying and decide on a DIY conveyance for the sale, you may experience difficulty when redeeming your current mortgage. Potential problems also arise concerning the deposit due from your buyer on exchange of contracts. The solicitor acting for the buyer is unlikely to advise his client to pay a deposit to you (rather than to your solicitor if you were using one). The concern would be that you might spend it, be declared bankrupt, or refuse to sell. You would not therefore be in a position to use the deposit from your sale as the deposit on your purchase (see Exchange of Contracts below), and would consequently need to find cash for the purpose.

A further problem arises when it comes to raising finance for a purchase. If you do your own conveyance you will almost certainly come up against opposition from lenders, to the extent that most of them would not even process a loan application without details of the borrower's solicitor.

If you are still keen to go it alone, consider first the type of transaction involved. A DIY purchase of a leasehold property is potentially fraught with difficulty, not least because of the unfathomable jargon used to word a lease, which may make it difficult for you to understand fully what you are agreeing to. But understand you must, to be sure the lease is sound and there are no unreasonable terms or service charges.

There are several books on the market which aim to give step-by-step instructions, but do make sure the one you choose is up to date, and bear in mind that it would be difficult in a book to cover every possible scenario or deal with every problem which could arise outside the scope of a 'normal' conveyance.

Joint purchases

Where two or more people buy a property together, they do so either as *joint tenants* or as *tenants in common*, which in legal jargon are the terms used to distinguish between those who co-own jointly and those who co-own separately. The term *tenant* does not mean that you only have a tenancy or lease of the premises, and it applies to freehold purchases as well.

• Joint Tenancy

This is the usual arrangement if you are buying as husband and wife, but can also be the case between unmarried couples and where there are more than two joint owners. Joint tenants own the whole of the property together, with no one having sole or greater ownership of any part. If one of the owners dies the other(s) 'inherit' automatically, so it is not possible for one party to leave a share of the property in a will to another person, or to sell his interest in his lifetime. It is irrelevant that one of the owners may make a greater contribution to the purchase than the other, or who pays the mortgage if there is one.

• Tenancy in Common

This arrangement protects a buyer who purchases with someone else and makes a greater financial contribution to the purchase. Each tenant has his own share of the property (not literally – if the owners decide to live in separate parts of the property that will be a personal arrangement between them). The proportion of interest each party has in the property is decided at the time of purchase, and this may not necessarily be in equal divisions. If, for example, one of the owners contributes twice as much of the purchase price as the other, he will receive twice as much of the proceeds in the event the property is sold, provided the deed of purchase sets out those proportions. Each owner can bequeath his interest in the property to another person since ownership does not automatically pass to the surviving owner(s) in the event of death.

The main point of drawing up either of the above agreements only really becomes relevant when the property is sold. This is especially so in the case of tenants in common, where the property will be sold even if only one of the owners wishes it. Should one or more refuse to sell, it is possible to apply to the courts for an order compelling the sale, and the courts can enforce the sale against the wishes of the co-owner who is reluctant to sell, unless the original arrangement, made formally, stipulated that the decision to sell must be agreed by both (or all) of the owners.

Similarly, in the case of a joint tenancy, if for example a married couple intend to go their separate ways and one of them wants to sell the property but the other doesn't, the property has to be sold, by obtaining a court order if necessary, although if there are children living in the family home, the courts may rule that the property is not sold until the youngest child is 18 years old. Alternatively, it may be possible for one of the owners to buy out the other and become the sole owner. The owner being bought out would have to agree to the purchase (and amount offered). The property would, on paper at least, be sold and then subsequently purchased, incurring many of the usual fees incurred in buying and selling a property. The sale proceeds would naturally be split equally, with the new sole owner funding the 50% needed to complete the purchase.

Making a purchase as a couple is a big step in any relationship, so the commitment needs to be long-term. Apart from the emotional turmoil and domestic upheaval when a property is sold because of a dissolved partnership between the owners, it could take time to find a buyer, and selling the property will incur substantial costs.

The legal process

The following information assumes the purchase is of a freehold property in England or Wales. In Scotland, some conveyance procedures are different, and are dealt with in the next chapter.

The mountain of paper used in each property purchase probably costs the life of a small tree, and you can expect to receive from your solicitor a stream of documents in need of signature and/or approval. The process mostly follows a set pattern with few deviations, but occasionally complications arise which are outside the scope of the schedule of events shown below.

Fixtures and Fittings

At the outset of a purchase you need to clarify exactly what, apart from the bricks and mortar, is included in the purchase price. The seller may be leaving carpets and curtains or he may strip the place down to the boards. Either is acceptable, as long as there is agreement between you and the seller about what will be left in the property as part of the purchase. You probably discussed this with the seller when you viewed the property, but for clarification your solicitor obtains written details from the seller showing which fixtures and fittings are included. The buyer receives a copy of this and should look through it carefully to make sure the seller has not gone back on what was agreed. If he retracts what was originally included in the sale, you should advise your solicitor accordingly. It could prove difficult to prove a verbal arrangement, and by this stage the seller will probably adopt a take-it-or-leave-it attitude, but it might be possible to renegotiate a reduction in the purchase price if the cost of the item under discussion is worth haggling over.

Some fixtures and fittings should automatically be included in the purchase price, like fitted cupboards, plumbing and wiring, and the plants in the garden, but other items like freestanding appliances (fridge, washing machine etc.), carpets and curtains are often removed by the seller as his personal possessions. Arguments can occur over some items which you might reasonably imagine would be left because they are fixed to the property, like shelves, curtain rails and wall lights, but which the seller does not have to leave behind, so it is important to clarify this one way or another.

The search

Your solicitor will send a local search application to the local authority, and usually receives a reply in around 10 days. The information supplied discloses such things as whether the property is a listed building and whether there are any road-widening schemes planned in the immediate vicinity, but not everything will be marked against the property. If you have any particular concerns it is imperative that you discuss them with your solicitor, who can then make further enquiries if necessary.

The search will also disclose whether the property has been granted planning permission for building work, and/or whether such work has had building regulations approval. If the property you are buying has a new porch, for example, it may have required planning permission. The rules are complex, so any new building work will need clarification. The seller should have to hand a Completion Certificate for work carried out on the property. This certificate is proof that the work meets building standards. If the seller does not have such documentation, he may instead have written confirmation that the work did *not* need planning permission or building regulations approval. If the seller cannot show consent or confirm that no future action will be taken over the work, you could be taking a serious risk in continuing with the purchase. If you try to sell the property in the future, this problem will almost certainly present itself again.

Your solicitor may pay for the search on your behalf and then seek reimbursement in his final account, or he may request payment from you for the search before applying for it.

Usually it is the solicitor acting for the buyer applies for the search, but occasionally a seller who is keen to proceed quickly applies for the search on his own property. This can save time when he finds a buyer, although the search is only valid for a limited period so he would have to be confident of a quick sale or risk losing the search fee.

Land Registry

When you begin the buying process, your solicitor receives from the seller's solicitor official copies of the entries about the property at the Land Registry, to make sure that the person you are buying from is the actual owner, and to obtain general details of the property and any charges upon it. Final searches from the Land Registry are also made after exchange of contracts but before completion, as protection for you. These searches give your solicitor time to register the title of the property in your name, so ensuring that the seller cannot sell the property to anyone else in the meantime.

The ownership (or title) of most property in England and Wales is now registered with the Land Registry. The Land Registry charges a fee for registration, based on the purchase price.

The contract

The seller's solicitor draws up a contract of sale, identifying the seller, the buyer and the property, and listing any conditions, such as the price, the amount of deposit you will need to supply at exchange of contracts, rights of access, confirmation of vacant possession, details of any restrictive covenants and, in the case of leaseholds, a copy of the lease. A copy of this contract is then sent to your solicitor (unsigned of course) for approval. If you and your solicitor approve the contract, you will then sign it and return it to your solicitor for retention until exchange of contracts (see below). At the time of sending out the contract, the seller's solicitor may also supply such documents as the NHBC certificate, planning consents, the fixtures-and-fittings form and the Preliminary Information Form.

Preliminary Information Form

Previously known as the preliminary enquiry form, this document is now in two parts. Part 1 is completed by the seller and part 2 by his solicitor, and the form is then sent to your solicitor, giving information on boundary fences, rights of access, notices, restrictions, guarantees, services etc. The seller is required to give truthful replies to the questions asked in the form or, if he does not know the answer, to say so. The form may therefore be littered with such vague answers as 'Don't know' or 'Not to my knowledge' which may not be sufficient. If anything in particular needs clarification, you will need to ask your solicitor to insist that the seller gives more specific answers.

Exchange of contracts

Once the Preliminary Information Form has been received and the contract approved and signed, a telephone call takes place between the solicitors acting for you and for the seller, confirming the terms, the deposit and the completion date. Both solicitors formally agree that they will uphold their client's part of the contract and post it that night. This is the exchange of contracts and once this takes place the commitment to buy/sell is binding.

You may already have discussed the anticipated completion date with the seller (either directly if the relationship allows, or indirectly through the agent or your solicitors), so you will already know roughly when you are likely to take ownership before exchange of contracts, but once contracts are exchanged the date for completion is formally set.

This is also the point at which you become liable to pay a deposit, usually 5-10% of the purchase price. It is common to use a deposit received on a sale as a deposit on a purchase, so if you are selling as well as purchasing, your solicitor uses the deposit paid by your buyer as the deposit on the property you are buying, as long as all parties agree. For example:

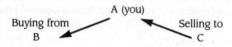

In this short chain, C is buying your home and you in turn are buying from B. As a first time buyer, C needs to raise the necessary funds for his deposit, which is sent to your solicitor with the signed contract. You do not usually need to supply funds personally to pay the deposit to B because your solicitor will bank your buyer's cheque (into a 'client' account) and then issue a cheque for the deposit you are liable for. The exception to this might be if B is demanding a higher deposit amount than your buyer is paying, perhaps because the property you are buying is more expensive than the one you are selling, so 5% of the selling price is less than 5% of the purchase price. In this case you may be required to make up the difference.

In some cases the deposit from C is paid direct to B if there is agreement from all parties. This makes little difference to you, since the amount you would receive from C would normally be indirectly paid over to B anyway. If you are a first time buyer (C in the above illustration), you will need to find cash for your deposit, since lenders do not fund this part of the purchase.

After exchange of contracts, you become liable for the property you are purchasing, although you have no right of occupation yet. In other words you must continue with the purchase even if the building burns down between now and completion, but you are not allowed to live there. Given your position, it is usual for you as buyer to insure the building from this date, and many mortgage companies automatically arrange cover from the date of exchange. However, if you are not borrowing, or are arranging your own insurance, you will need to organize this yourself.

The period between exchange of contracts and completion used to be around 4 weeks, but is now more often 2 weeks. If there is a chain which has taken a long time to put together, the period could be even shorter because you and the seller will not want any further delays. It is more common for a completion date to be delayed than brought forward, usually because essential documents have not been received in time.

Discharging the mortgage

If you are simultaneously selling and buying, your existing mortgage will need to be redeemed (repaid). To do this, your solicitor requests a redemption figure from your present lenders, which is the amount needed to discharge the mortgage on completion of the sale – in other words the amount you still owe. Although it is usual for the solicitor handling the conveyance to deal with redemption of the mortgage, sometimes the lenders employs a solicitor to undertake the redemption, in which case there will be another bill to settle.

Some lenders penalize early repayment of mortgages by charging a mortgage redemption fee which can be equivalent to several months' interest. This usually only applies if you took advantage of an incentive offered by the lenders at the start of your mortgage (e.g. a fixed rate, discount or cash-back arrangement), and are repaying the mortgage within the first years. This fee can often be avoided by taking out a new mortgage with the same lenders. However, the sale and purchase may need to be conducted within a limited space of time, which may not be possible if you intend to sell the existing property first, then have a leisurely look for the next one whilst in temporary accommodation. You should confirm this with your lenders.

Requisitions on title

The seller will be asked by his solicitor to confirm that there have been no changes in the replies to the Preliminary Information Form between the time they were supplied and before completion takes place. The seller also supplies an undertaking to redeem any existing mortgage on the property and confirm that the property will be vacant on completion (*vacant possession*).

Transfer

A draft transfer will be sent by your solicitor to the seller's solicitor. Once approved, it is 'engrossed', i.e. typed on good quality paper in readiness for execution, and then sent to the seller (via his solicitor) for signature and return. This form shows the seller(s) by name, the property address, the purchase price and the name of the buyer(s), and any special conditions or covenants affecting the property. Once returned by the seller to his solicitor, it will be held by him until the completion date.

Completion

Completion should take place on the date specified at exchange of contracts. This basically means that the deeds to the property are transferred to you (or to your lenders if you have a mortgage or other loan secured on the property) in exchange for the purchase price. In most cases, the buyer and seller contribute very little to the day of completion, but your solicitor should advise once completion has taken place, so that you know you can then obtain entry to the property.

Solicitors acting for buyer and seller do not usually physically meet in the bank lobby or office of the lenders or each other, and on behalf of their clients hand over documents in exchange for a bankers' draft. Instead, and not nearly so dramatic, completion is provided for in the Requisition on the Title in that you give undertakings, or there are implied undertakings, that you will pay over the purchase money. As soon as this money is received by the seller's solicitor, he will send to your solicitor (usually by that night's post) the documents which have been signed, sealed and properly executed to pay off any existing mortgage on the property. Your solicitor does not then get the papers on the day of completion. In practical terms, what happens is that on the morning of completion the seller's solicitor must be in receipt of the signed transfer documents. Your solicitor will telephone the seller's solicitor and confirm that he has the funds and is now putting them in the telegraphic transfer (the bank system for transfer of money). The seller's solicitor either accepts that and release the keys (or gives the seller or his agents the okay to do so), or insists on waiting until the funds are actually received in his bank before releasing the keys. In this case, once confirmation is received from the bank (by telephone usually) that the funds are received, the seller's solicitor telephones his client and/or the selling agent or seller to say that keys can be released to you.

Literally speaking, the seller should leave a key to the property with his solicitor, who will hand it to you once completion has taken place. In practice, most sellers leave a key with the estate agent who handled the sale, or alternatively with a neighbour. Naturally you need to make sure you know where to collect the key from, in advance of completion day, and it is worth asking the seller to label any cupboard keys so that the buyer knows what they are for.

As far as you are concerned, once you hear from your solicitor to say that completion has taken place, you can congratulate yourself as the new owner and move in.

Failure to complete

Occasionally, a buyer may find that he is unable to complete the purchase on the date specified in the contract. This may be, for example, because his purchase funds are not available in time, and if this happens you could find yourself liable to pay interest to the seller on the outstanding amount. A completion notice will be served on you, calling for completion of the transaction within a set period (14 days usually), and if you cannot meet this deadline you stand to lose your deposit and the property, which the seller can re-sell to someone else. If sold later at a price less than the original purchase price (less deposit), you may also be required to make up the difference.

If it is the seller who holds up the transaction, you can instigate legal proceedings to complete the transaction.

Conveyance of new homes

If you are buying a newly built home or one still under construction, some of the conveyancing procedures will be different from the norm.

Searches

Your solicitor will carry out a search through the local authority in the usual way, but while the search may show planning permission granted for the estate, e.g. '50 dwellings', it may not show permission on adjoining land for further building.

If the builder of your new home, usually a company, has mortgaged the site, which is commonly the case, your solicitor will obtain an undertaking prior to completion that the plot being purchased will be released by the building company's mortgagees on completion.

Purchase Deed

Purchase deeds relating to properties on a large estate are usually identical, requiring all buyers to comply with the same restrictive covenants, most probably restricting use of the property to a private dwelling only and requiring buyers to obtain consent before altering the building. The law may in such cases allow one owner on the estate to enforce the restrictions against an adjoining owner even though there is no direct agreement between them.

The contract

The expected date for completion of construction is entered on the contract, or a provision made, such as 10 days' notice of completion, along with confirmation that the builder is registered with the NHBC or equivalent. The builder's obligation to maintain the roads on site until they are adopted by the local authority will also be included. Copy details of the agreement between local authority and builder concerning roads will usually be sent with the contract, together with details of planning permission.

Your lenders will usually need to re-inspect the property before the purchase funds are released, and may charge you a fee for this inspection. Keeping your solicitor informed, and depositing with him the lenders' re-inspection fee can help to avoid a last-minute rush.

Finances

Aside from the cost of the property itself, buying your own home is a very expensive business. There are ways of saving money – you could do your own removals for a start – but most of the costs are unavoidable and it can seem that charges and fees result at every turn.

Some of the fees will be payable before the purchase is completed. Your lenders may charge an application and/or reservation fee, and you will need to pay for a valuation or survey. Your solicitor may ask for advance payment of the local search fee, although he would not normally expect payment for his time and expertise until the transaction is completed.

Fees encountered if you are selling as well as buying are paid out by your solicitor from the proceeds of your sale, and include settlement of the estate agency fee, the solicitor's own charges, and costs incurred in searches, land registry fees, stamp duty etc. You should confirm with your solicitor the fee you have agreed with the estate agent, allowing for VAT. Some agents stipulate in their agency agreements that their fee is payable on exchange of contracts, but most are happy to wait until completion.

On top of the many fees, you will encounter costs in setting up your new home. You may need carpets or curtains if these are not included in the purchase, not to mention furniture, and sundry costs like change-of-address cards and stamps, which all add up. You may also face charges for services to the property: a connection fee for the telephone or security payment for gas supply, for example.

There will probably be a hundred and one items you would like to buy, so you need to think carefully about what is most important to you – it may not be the most sensible, but if it gives you pleasure, who cares? My own experience taught me that silver-grey carpet throughout a small flat is not practical (you live and learn), but at the time such a luxury seemed far more important than mundane items like furniture, and I entertained friends just as well without a dining table and chairs, though in retrospect some plates might have been nice, and given the colour of the carpet, a doormat would certainly have been useful!

Once the purchase has been completed, or maybe a day or so before, your solicitor will send an invoice showing his charges, any fees incurred, and the money needed to complete the purchase (see sample invoice below). Cleared funds must be in the solicitor's client account by the day of completion. The solicitor is prevented by his professional body from drawing against uncleared cheques, so make sure he has the funds available in time.

BRADLEY & CO. SOLICITORS

Mr & Mrs Buyer

INVOICE

PURCHASE OF 22 BISHOPS AVENUE

	£	£
Purchase price		54,000.00
ADD:		
Our professional charges	295.00	
VAT @ 17.5%	51.63	
PAID:		
Local search fee	56.00	
Official search fee	2.00	
Land Registry fees (not yet paid)	140.00	
Telegraphic Transfer fee	30.00	
	————	
		574.63
		54,574.63
DEDUCT:		
Mortgage Advance	35,000.00	
Less Remittance fee	20.00	
	————	
		(34,980.00)
Balance due to complete purchase		£19,594.63

This example shows that Mr and Mrs Buyer need to find the balance of £19,594.63 to complete the purchase, part of which they have already given over as the deposit on exchange of contracts. Since Mr & Mrs Buyer are also selling (see next sample invoice), they put the proceeds from their sale towards the purchase, reducing the amount needed to complete the transaction to £1,130.26. They need to send this amount to their solicitor several days before completion so that he has sufficient cleared funds for the purchase. If there had been a surplus of funds, because the property being purchased was much cheaper than that being sold, the solicitor would issue a cheque for the balance within a day or two of completion.

BRADLEY & CO. SOLICITORS

Mr & Mrs Buyer

INVOICE

SALE OF 'THE NOOK'

	£	£
Sale price		50,000.00
DEDUCT:		
Our professional charges	295.00	
VAT @ 17.5%	51.63	
PAID:		
Estate Agents	1,175.00	
Mortgage Redemption	30,000.00	
Office Copies	14.00	
	———	31,535.63
		18,464.37
Less balance due to complete purchase		(19,594.63)
Balance due		£1,130.26

117

Had the purchase price been in excess of £60,000, Mr & Mrs Buyer would have had the added expense of Stamp Duty to pay. Stamp Duty is a tax on documents rather than transactions, payable on the transfer of certain assets (land can only be transferred by document). The current rate is 1%, payable on sales of land and leases valued above the £60,000 threshold.

7. BUYING IN SCOTLAND

The procedure for buying property in Scotland differs from that elsewhere in the UK. In particular, when you make an offer to buy a property (unless it is newly built), you do so in direct competition with other prospective buyers. Furthermore, a binding contract to buy and sell is entered into at a much earlier stage in Scotland than in England and Wales, and the subsequent conveyance procedure is considerably shorter. The time from acceptance of an offer to settlement of the sale is generally four to five weeks, compared with about 12 weeks elsewhere.

In Scotland, gazumping is not a feature of home buying because contracts become binding once they are agreed. Similarly, a buyer cannot reduce the agreed price ('gazunder') once contracts are agreed.

Finding your home

If you want to buy a new home, you should contact the builder direct, or the builder's sales agent if he is using one (see Chapter 4). You will find advertisements for new homes in the local papers, on television and through Scotland's New Homebuyer, a quarterly magazine available free from building societies, banks, solicitors' property centres and estate agents.

Older homes are advertised in the local papers by estate agents, solicitors and private individuals. Solicitors in Scotland have an added role to play in the purchase and sale of property, since they have traditionally acted as selling agents. So as well as through estate agents, you may also find the home you are looking for through the various solicitor-based marketing services like solicitors' property centres, who act for the solicitors who subscribe to them. These centres differ from estate agents in that once you express an interest in a property, they hand you on to the seller's solicitor who handles any further enquiries.

Making an offer

Most houses and flats are sold through a system of 'blind bidding'. The seller sets a price, which is usually the minimum he or she expects to achieve, and then asks for offers over that price. If and when there is sufficient interest, a *closing date* (see below) is set for the submission of offers. How much you will have to pay will depend on how much competition there is from other potential buyers. If the offer you make at the closing date is not successful, you will not get an opportunity to submit a higher one unless, for some reason, the contract with the successful bidder falls through.

Sometimes property is advertised at a fixed price if there is little activity in the market or the seller is looking for a quick sale. The first offer at that price is usually accepted. This is also the usual procedure for newly-built homes.

If you are seriously interested in a particular property, you should arrange a valuation and survey, and get agreement in principal from your lenders to your borrowing requirements. At the same time, you should notify your interest to the seller's solicitor so that you will be told if a closing date for offers is set. The number of surveys instructed by different prospective buyers is a good indication of the likely competition, so ask the seller about this.

Valuations and surveys

Your lenders will want a mortgage valuation report for their benefit, before you make an offer on a property. You can also instruct a surveyor to carry out a Homebuyer's Survey and Valuation. As your report will contain an opinion about the value of the property, find out beforehand whether your lenders will accept this valuation for lending purposes. If they will (which is usual), this will save you paying the lenders' valuation fee as well.

A building survey is rarely used in Scotland, partly because of the speed of buying and selling, and partly because most sellers are unlikely to allow such a survey (because it often involves such disruption as taking up floorboards etc.) unless there is a very limited market for the property and you have expressed a very strong interest.

While you may have to instruct a number of surveys before you make a successful bid for a property, you will be making your offer with knowledge of the state of the property and its value to you. Your surveyor is a good source of information on the local property market but his valuation will not necessarily indicate how much you will need to bid to secure a purchase. You may find, for example, that the surveyor values a particular property at £60,000 for the actual structure, when the seller is inviting offers over £62,000 and expects to achieve somewhere around £67,000 because properties of that type are in demand.

Closing dates

When there is sufficient interest in the property, the seller's agent sets a closing date. This is a specific time and date by which offers should be made. If you have expressed interest through your solicitor or by having a survey carried out, you will be told about the closing date. It is not in the seller's interests to set a closing date that does not allow time for all interested parties to arrange their valuations and surveys and prepare their offers, so you should have plenty of time to get organized.

There is nothing to stop you making an offer at any time before or after a closing date is set. However, if there is interest from other prospective buyers, and the setting of a closing date will show that there is, your offer is likely to be rejected and you will have revealed your hand.

Once you have decided how much you are prepared (and can afford) to offer, your solicitor submits your blind bid in competition with the other potential buyers. The offers remain sealed until the set time on the closing date. The seller does not have to accept the highest offer, or any offer, but he usually will unless it has unacceptable conditions attached. If the seller accepts your offer, it then proceeds to the *missives* (see below).

If a closing date is not set, this may indicate that there is little interest in the property and the seller may be open to negotiation on the price.

Missives

Your offer to buy, and the seller's acceptance, are normally made through your respective solicitors. The offer and acceptance take the form of an exchange of letters known as *missives*.

Your offer should include a brief description of the property, the proposed date of entry and the agreed price. It will also mention any specific items that you want included in the sale, such as carpets and curtains, and will include a number of conditions. The conditions, which will vary from sale to sale, are designed to ensure, for example, that the property has no unreasonable planning restrictions on it, that any alterations have the necessary planning permissions and building-control consents, that there are no outstanding statutory notices or planning proposals affecting it, that any relevant guarantees will be produced, and that the seller is genuinely the owner of the property and that his or her right to sell it is not restricted in any way.

The seller's solicitor may accept your offer as it is, or make a qualified acceptance, asking for the deletion or variance of some of your conditions. This process may involve a number of missives over a few days. Once there is agreement, the missives are concluded and you have a binding contract.

The legal process

Once the missives are concluded, your solicitor will proceed with the conveyancing, which is the legal process of transferring the title of the property from the seller to you. You should arrange the following:

- Mortgage and life insurance. If you need mortgage funding, you will need to make an application to your lenders, and make sure that any linked life insurance is in hand.
- Buildings insurance. You should make sure that the property is adequately insured, as the seller's insurance may not be adequate.
- Title – if you are buying with a spouse or partner, you should decide how you wish the title deeds to be prepared, as this may affect a will made in the past or in the future. Your solicitor will advise.

Your solicitor will investigate the property and its title. This includes:

- finding out about any limitations or legal restrictions (*burdens*) or obligations (*servitudes*) that affect the property;

- checking the rights of the *superior* – a person or company who has retained some rights from the property's original sale;
- making sure that the ground burdens, such as factor's fees and maintenance charges, are properly divided between you and the seller;
- redeeming the *feu duty* (a periodic payment to the superior) if applicable.

Standard security

This is a legal agreement that grants security over the property to the lenders. It has to be drawn up by a solicitor. If your lenders will agree to your solicitor doing this, it will be slightly cheaper. When it is ready, you will have to sign it.

Occupancy rights

Your solicitor will check that there are no outstanding rights on the property that could affect the transfer of ownership to you. If you are married but the home is to be in your name only, your solicitor must get your spouse's consent to grant the standard security to the lenders.

The disposition

This is the document that transfers the property from the seller to you. A draft document is drawn up and agreed between your respective solicitors. The seller signs it before the settlement, so that the disposition, deeds and keys can be exchanged for the full purchase price on the date of entry.

Settlement

Your solicitor will certify to your lenders that the title is good, and get the loan cheque from your lenders and any contribution required from you. In exchange for the cheque for the purchase price, your solicitor receives the disposition, other title deeds and the keys. The property is then yours.

Registration

Your ownership of the property and the standard security in favour of your lenders will either be recorded in the Register of Sasines or registered in the Land Register of Scotland, depending on where you live. The Land Register will replace the Register of Sasines by the year 2003.

Tenements and multi-occupancy buildings

If you buy a flat, you will have some responsibility for the repair and maintenance of shared areas and services and their costs. Usually, your title deeds will set out the common areas of the building you can use and for which you are responsible, your share of the costs, and how decisions should be reached among the various owners.

Many tenement flats, especially in Glasgow and the West of Scotland, have a *factor* or agent to look after repairs and maintenance. This is also popular in modern blocks of flats throughout Scotland. Factors are firms that specialize in maintaining multiple-ownership properties. Generally, they inspect the property at least once a year and arrange for any common repairs to be carried out. The owners are billed either twice or four times a year for the factor's fees and any common repair costs. For large or expensive repairs, the factor may require prior approval from all the owners and advance payment. You do not have to have a factor unless it is required by the title deeds. If all the owners agree, you can arrange your own maintenance and repairs. Similarly, you can appoint a factor or change a factor.

8. MOVING

Buying a home is exciting, rewarding and a chance for new beginnings, but as the date for moving looms ever closer, tension and stress can mar the pleasure. Happily, much of the stress can be reduced with advance planning, and if you make yourself fully aware of every step of the buying process you can usually take action to avoid any nasty surprises. Last-minute complications are the bane of every home move, but if you are well prepared and keep track of everything you can usually sort them out before a minor hiccup turns into a major problem.

It is impossible to prepare for every eventuality, and pondering too long on what *might* go wrong during a move is a sure way to spoil the whole experience. However, it is necessary to embark upon some simple preparations if moving day has any hope of proceeding smoothly, and you will need to call on all your reserves of patience to deal calmly with the inevitable upheaval.

Something which comes as a shock to many people is that moving a lifetime's collection of possessions from one place to another is physically demanding. If you hire a van for a DIY move, you will probably handle every item yourself at least four times – into a box or crate, on to the van, off the van, then out of the box or crate. Even if you hire a removals company to pack as well as transport furniture and effects, there will still be an element of packing to be done on the day, not to mentioning cleaning the new home, keeping children occupied and supplying refreshments for yourself and the removal men or helpers. Even for the well prepared, moving day is a tiring experience, only survived by good organization and a bit of luck. For those who make no preparation, chaos and confusion are inevitable.

Moving day should be a time to reap the benefits of all the hard work put into finding and arranging the purchase of the new home, and with a bit of effort beforehand, it can be.

Advance preparations

Throughout the time it takes to complete the purchase, you are well advised to keep in close contact with both your solicitor and the selling agents, to make sure everything is proceeding smoothly; that all relevant information has been obtained and dealt with in good time, and that everyone involved has done what is required of them. Some knowledge of the buying system enables you to chart the progress of your house-buying and draw attention to potential delays, so try to keep ahead of schedule and don't feel shy of chasing up the surveyor, or of prompting your solicitor. Usually they have everything under control, but what is just all in the day's work to them is vitally important to you.

Once contracts for the purchase have been exchanged (or in Scotland, once missives have been concluded), the date for completion (in Scotland, settlement) is known. Under either system, you should by this time have discussed with your solicitor any preference regarding moving dates, so that the arrangements are convenient to both you and the seller.

Once the legal paperwork is on target for completion, you can begin the task of transferring services and advising those who need to know of the move, including the following:

- Insurance company
- Bank
- Milkman
- Vet
- DVLC – vehicle registration/driving licence (but don't forget you will need to produce your driving licence if hiring a van for the move)
- TV Licensing Authority
- Rental/HP companies
- Doctor, dentist and optician
- Tax Office
- Local council
- Solicitor and other professional advisors
- Employer/work colleagues

In most cases all you need to do is to send a brief note, showing your full name, the address you are moving from, the address you are moving to, and any reference number. Keep a copy of the letters so that you know who has been advised, or make a list of who you have written to and when, and keep that instead. Friends and family also need to be advised. This can involve a great many letters, so you might find it easier to have 'change of address' cards printed, or buy pads of pre-printed notes which just need the new address and phone number written in.

Packing is obviously something to be done in advance of moving day, and this is dealt with later, but there are other jobs you can do in advance which often get overlooked until the last minute. It is a good idea to make a list of these so that you do not leave yourself a mountain of things to do the night before you move. There are bound to be some last-minute chores, but the less you have to do on the day, the better. If that means eating out on the last evening in your old home, or picnicking on a take-away in the only room left with curtains and somewhere to sit, then this is a far better option than having to clear the kitchen or take down fittings the next day when you will have quite enough to do as it is.

Countdown to moving day

As far ahead as you can manage:
  • Take cuttings of favourite garden plants, or divide them (you should not remove the whole plant)

Two weeks before moving day:
  • Order pet tags with new address
  • Arrange for disconnection of appliances, e.g. gas fires or cooker to take place on moving day

One week before moving day:
  • Collect any dry cleaning
  • Return library books (if moving to a different area)
  • Dismantle structures as necessary, e.g. greenhouse, wardrobes

Two days before moving day:
- Defrost fridge and/or freezer

The day before moving day:
- Take down curtains and poles (if not included in the sale)
- Remove any fittings not included in the sale, e.g. light fittings
- Roll up rugs
- Make sure your car has enough petrol

First-time buyers leaving home will also need to embark on a shopping trip to buy essentials like crockery, cutlery, cleaning tools, etc. If you are moving from rented accommodation, you will need to give the required notice to your landlord.

Transferring services

If you are taking on services for the first time, some suppliers may insist that you pay a connection charge or security deposit before they will accept you as a customer. Most of the following information concerning the connection of services applies to first-time buyers as well as existing customers, but if you have not owned your home before it might be worth giving the supplier more than the minimum required notice to allow time for applications to be processed.

• Telephone

British Telecom can transfer your existing telephone number to the new property (if the area code is the same) on the day of the move, and this is obviously very useful. The current charge for this is £30.50 plus VAT. In order for BT to arrange this service you must give at least two weeks' notice by contacting the operator (on 150) and giving your details. If you are moving out of the area covered by your existing code, either you will be given a new telephone number for your new address, or, as usually happens, you can take over the one used by the present owners unless they are transferring it to their new address. Contact the telephone operator, tell them your existing number and the address you are moving to. They will then send you the necessary forms for completion, advise how much their charge will be, and issue your new number. If your service is not from BT but through an alternative system like Mercury, or if you use a pager or mobile phone, you need to contact the relevant companies who supply the services, although most mobile-phone users will naturally continue to use their existing number.

TAKE A TIP
If you know your new telephone number in advance, it can be included on your change-of-address cards.

If your new property does not already have a telephone, arranging connection is simply a matter of telephoning the operator with your details (on 150), giving seven days' notice of a convenient connection date. British Telecom currently charges £99 plus VAT for the installation of a new line. This charge appears on your first bill in full, or alternatively you can ask to pay by instalments, in which case you pay a £25 deposit and then further charges of £25 are included on the next four bills, which makes the instalment method rather more expensive. In addition, there is a charge of £21.86 for line rental, payable 3 months in advance. The line rental is an on-going expense and appears on each bill. If you rent the handset, this will cost £4.99 each quarter, but you have the option of buying your own instrument and avoiding this rental payment.

• Council Tax

When you know where you will be moving to, and when, contact the council to whom you presently pay Council Tax. Advise them of your current address the date you will be vacating it, and the address you are moving to. The council will calculate the relevant daily charge for the time you remain in your existing property, and then open a new account for your new property if it is within their governing area. If you are moving to a different part of the country, you need to contact the local authority there.

MOVING

• Electricity

The electricity company which supplies your power needs at least 2 working days' notice of your intended move. This is the minimum notice you are allowed to give by law, but ideally you should give at least a week. Write or telephone, giving your account number and the address of the property. If you are moving on a weekday, the electricity company can arrange to read the meter on the day you move out. The account can then be closed and the final bill sent to your new address. Similarly, a meter-reader will call at your new address (if this has been arranged) to take that reading, for which the previous owners are then billed, and a new account for the property is opened in your name. If you are moving over the weekend, the process is much the same but instead of the electricity company taking the meter readings, you should make a note of readings yourself, at both the property you are vacating (before you leave), and the property you move to (on arrival). Write to, or telephone, the electricity company with both readings so that final billing can be arranged for each account.

• Gas

If any gas appliances, such as the cooker, need to be disconnected before you move, arrange an appointment in advance otherwise you may have to leave the appliance where it is until it can be disconnected, which would be very inconvenient. The system of transferring the account and meter readings is much the same as for electricity (see above).

If you use gas cylinders rather than mains gas, any appliances not included in the sale need to be carefully disconnected, and the cylinders turned off. The cylinders might be left behind for use by the new owners, or returned to the supplier to reclaim any deposit paid.

• Water

When you know your moving date, advise the company which supplies your water. Tell them your current address, the address you are moving to, and the date of the move. The company then prepares a final bill for your current address, calculating the daily charges to the last day of occupation. If you are moving within the same supply area, it also opens an account for your new address. If you are moving to a different supply area, contact the relevant company and advise the date from which you will be taking on the service. If you have a water meter, this needs to be read, so contact the water company in the same way but ask it also to arrange for a meter reading. If the new property has a water meter, ask the water company to read the meter on the day you move in, or take the reading yourself on arrival.

• Post

Your local post office can arrange for your mail to be redirected. You may think you have advised everyone of your new address, but being sure all your mail is automatically redirected gives peace of mind in case someone has been overlooked. You can apply for redirection by completing the appropriate form available in post offices or by telephoning 01345-777888. The charge for this service depends on the length of time redirection is arranged (1 month, 3 months or 1 year) and is applied to each different surname, e.g. Mr & Mrs Jones would be charged one fee for both people, whereas Mr Green and Mr Smith would be charged a fee each.

Insurance

> **TAKE A TIP**
> Moving home is often the time to evaluate your insurance arrangements. Some companies offer incentives to new customers which they do not broadcast to their existing clients, so it might be worth looking around for a better quote as a new customer rather than remaining with a company which is taking your continued custom for granted.

Most removal and storage companies arrange insurance policies on request to cover for loss or damage incurred during a move, but before going to the extra expense of taking out a policy with them, it is worth checking with the company which insures your contents to see if you already have cover. If not, your insurer may be able to extend your current policy to give adequate cover, although you may be charged an additional premium. Whether you take out insurance through a removals company or extend your existing policy, read the small print to check the amount and conditions of cover. Be aware that it is common practice to exclude 'owner packed' goods, which could leave many of your most precious possessions uninsured. Insurance policies which cover goods during removal frequently stipulate a time limit for making a claim. Because of this, even if you do not unpack all your possessions immediately, they should at least be checked for breakage once they are delivered.

> **DID YOU KNOW?** *Insurance cover offered by removal companies is not necessarily on a 'new for old' replacement basis, but is rather a reimbursement based on market value.*

If you hire a van to do the move yourself, you will need to pay for insurance (probably arranged by the van hire company) to cover loss or damage to the vehicle, and this insurance can carry a large excess figure (the part of any repair costs you would have to pay). If you borrow a van privately, from a friend or relative, make sure you are adequately insured to drive it. Instant cover is usually just a phone call away, but you should not assume the owner's insurance will cover you.

You may find that moving into a new area affects your existing car insurance, since different areas attract different premium rates.

If you buy any new furniture for your new home, advise your insurers, who may need to top up your existing cover.

Packing

> **TAKE A TIP**
> Before packing away tools, compile an emergency tool kit to
> cope with any small jobs at the other end. Include string, a
> sharp knife, screwdriver, hammer, fuses and a torch.

If you are doing all the packing yourself, and not employing a removal company to do it for you, it is advisable to start the job of packing into boxes or crates at least two weeks before the moving date, because you can be fairly sure that it will take longer than anticipated.

Rather than moving from room to room packing everything as you go, it is better to pack non-essentials first, especially those things which you will not be in a hurry to unpack at the other end. That way you can pack away a lot of things which are not used on a daily basis well in advance of the moving date, and leave these boxes unpacked at the other end until you decide at your leisure where to put the contents.

It is useful to label boxes as you pack, so that you know what is in them. You may initially remember what each box holds, but as more and more are filled and sealed it can start to get confusing. If you need to retrieve something which has already been packed, you can bet it will be in the last box you look in. However, only label boxes sufficiently to distinguish a box of shoes from a box of books, because trying to list each item in every box would be tedious and time-consuming.

Identify on your box labels the room where the contents came from. By labelling boxes 'Johnny's room', 'study' etc., you ensure that they can be unloaded straight into the right room at the new home, and you do not waste time and energy moving them again. For this system to work, the removal men need to know what each room in the new home is to be used for, since it may not be apparent to them which room you will be using as the dining room and which as the sitting room. The easiest way to indicate this is to draw up a simple floor plan of the new home. You can then name each room 'sitting room', 'bedroom 1', etc. on the plan, and label boxes accordingly.

TAKE A TIP

To see what kitchen equipment can be packed in advance and what needs to be available until the last minute, prepare an average day's meals, but don't put anything you use back in the cupboards. This pile of pans, crockery and cutlery left out will be what you use regularly; the rest can be packed away.

Packing is a good opportunity to sort out accumulated junk and take old clothes which haven't been worn for years to the local charity shop. If time allows, it is obviously better to do this when packing rather than moving everything and then sorting it out at the other end. Even after a ruthless clear-out you will need plenty of boxes or crates – probably double what you anticipate using. You could ask your local supermarket for some of the boxes their deliveries arrive in. Some removal firms supply boxes, but they often have to be emptied on arrival at the delivery address so that the driver can take them back to the depot, or else a rental charge is made.

Care should be taken to ensure that boxes containing fragile items are marked accordingly so that they are not loaded on to the removal van under a pile of heavier boxes, and the 'right way up' should be clearly displayed. Some sort of padding will be needed, so ask neighbours or friends to save their newspapers, and you could also utilize spare bedding, especially pillows, to cushion against damage.

It is a good idea to mark one box 'Do Not Remove' and put into this anything you do not want to go in the removal van, including for example:

- Kettle and tea things (a carton of UHT milk can be packed in advance since it does not require refrigeration until opened)
- Light bulbs/candles/torch
- Toilet roll, soap and a towel
- Cleaning materials
- Quick food (sandwiches, biscuits etc.)
- Small amount of cash
- Children's favourite toys
- Dog's favourite bone
- Telephone number of solicitor, selling agents etc., just in case there is a problem.

If you arrive at the new address before the removals van, which is likely, it might also be useful to transport the vacuum cleaner separately so that the carpets can be cleaned before they are covered up with furniture and boxes.

> **DID YOU KNOW?** *Freezers and fridges must be transported upright and should be left to stand in their new position for at least two hours before being switched on again (refer to manufacturer's handbook).*

If a removal firm is packing for you, they may come the day before the move to pack, then return on the day to load up. This is because they know that moving day is not the time to be frantically filling boxes and crates, so take note of their experience and make sure that, as far as possible, everything is packed by the eve of the move. Items which are in use until the last minute (bedding, toiletries etc.) take enough time to clear away without adding to them with non-essentials.

When the van arrives, it makes sense to synchronize the loading so that those things, such as carpets and rugs, which are needed first at the other end go into the van last. The removal men should do this for you, but it is worth bringing it to their attention.

If you are using a removal firm and not travelling in the van yourself, you will still need to transport yourself, your family, pets, and whatever you do not want to go in the van, by other means. If you do not have a car, it might be worth borrowing or hiring one for the day, since you could find yourself making several trips to drop the children off with friends, collect the keys, etc. etc.

Removals

Hiring a professional removal firm can be expensive. Whether you choose this option, as opposed to hiring a van and doing it yourself, depends on the distance involved, how fit you are, how much furniture you have to move and whether much of it is heavy or awkward to shift.

> **DID YOU KNOW?** *Unless you hold an HGV (heavy goods vehicle) driving licence, the size of van you are permitted to hire will be no more than 7.5 tonnes laden weight.*

DIY moving is usually cheaper, but the disadvantages should not be overlooked, and these can outweigh the monetary saving (which may only be small in any event if you shop around):

- Loading and unloading will take longer since you are unlikely to be as experienced as the removal staff.
- You will probably need to make more than one journey because the van will be too small to take everything in one go, and you will not be experienced enough to fully use the space available.
- You are more likely to damage something because you will not be adept at loading and handling. Removal men may appear to take less care than you would yourself, but their experience counts in loading and packing to avoid damage.
- It is physically strenuous – washing machines and wardrobes are even heavier than they look.
- It is emotionally more exhausting because you have more to think about.
- Negotiating stairs etc. with heavy goods may need lifting gear which you do not have.
- Any last minute jobs (and you can assume there some) will cause delays if you are preoccupied with loading and unloading.

TAKE A TIP

If you hire a van and move a long distance, bear in mind that you will probably have to bring the van back to where you hired it from, necessitating extra travelling.

If you decide to use a removal firm, get several quotes before making a choice. The standard of service varies between companies, and so does the price. Large companies offer a more comprehensive service than just transporting packed boxes from one place to another, and often give their clients the option of a full packing service, or at the very least, supply boxes and advice on packing etc. Inevitably the cost of this is built into the charge. A chap with a van will just arrive on the day with his vehicle and the muscle to load and unload, but the advantage is that he will be fairly cheap.

You do not need to limit your choice of removal company to those which operate where you currently live. You could instead use a company from the area you are moving to since the travelling for them is just the same. This can save you money if you are moving from, say, London to Cornwall, because the Cornish-based companies are likely to charge less than the London ones.

Before supplying a quote, an assessor from the removal company will normally visit to assess the amount of furniture and effects to be moved. Be sure to disclose everything (including the contents of loft, garage, garden shed), otherwise you may find the van they send is too small. If the move is likely to involve special requirements (perhaps because access at the other end is difficult for the van, or there are a lot of stairs for the removal men to negotiate), mention this to the assessor. Once you find a quote that is acceptable, confirm in writing any special requirements you have discussed, so that there is no argument about these later.

The amount of notice needed to book a removal firm varies: some only need a week, whereas others ask for a month. Friday and Saturday are the most popular days for moving, and the end of the month is always busy, so try to avoid these if you can. Moving over the weekend can cause problems if the emergency services of a plumber or electrician are needed, since they may not be available, and if they are, their fee will be higher than during the week. Bear in mind also that your solicitor's office will be closed.

Payment for removals is usually requested in advance. Some firms accept payment on the day, although they may ask for a deposit up front to secure the availability of a van and driver on the planned date. If you pay in cash, make sure you get a receipt from the driver. You may decide to give the removal men a tip, but this is not compulsory, and certainly if you have any cause for complaint you should not do so, since a tip would be construed as an indication of complete satisfaction on your part, and any later complaint or claim for damage may be viewed with suspicion.

Removal men often arrive very early in the morning, so if you are not an early riser be prepared for a rude awakening. Loading the contents of an average 3-bedroom house or flat takes in excess of three hours (all owing for frequent tea breaks), so the aim is to clear the property by noon, in time for the arrival of the new owners and their removal van. By the time you arrive at your new home, the previous owners are with any luck on the way to their new home, and so on.

Moving out

Once everything has been loaded on to the van, but before it departs to your new home, take a careful look around to make sure nothing has been forgotten. Sometimes the most obvious thing gets left behind (like a picture or rug) because it is seen so often that it becomes part of the decoration and does not stand out as removable. Also, things which are out of sight for most of the time, like the contents of the garage or loft, can be overlooked.

Turn off the heating (if that is what you have arranged with the new owners), make sure all the windows are closed and the entrance doors are locked, and take any necessary meter readings for connected services like gas and electricity. If you are using removal men, make sure they have the correct address of your new home, giving directions (perhaps including a sketchmap) as necessary.

If you are moving locally, unloading can probably be completed during the afternoon. If you are moving a long way, the removal company may unload the day after loading, so you will need to arrange overnight accommodation unless you are happy to spend the first night in your new home without any furniture. Discuss this with the removal company when its services are booked.

Moving in

Having prepared the process for moving your goods out of your old home, you now have to arrange the smooth moving in to the new one.

The removal van will probably take longer than you to arrive, giving you time to have a cup of tea and something to eat before starting the unloading and unpacking. When you get to your new home, take a good look round the property to make sure everything which should have been left by the previous owners has indeed been left, and if there are any omissions speak to your solicitor. If the central heating has been turned off, you might like to get this running, but in any event check that the heating and other appliances are working. If you have arranged for the connection of appliances and for meter readings you can expect a stream of callers. If you have not arranged for meter readings to be taken by the suppliers concerned, make a note of them yourself rather than relying on the previous owners to have done so.

Assuming you arranged for a telephone service to be connected, the telephone should be working, but if on arrival you are faced with a dead line, it will be necessary to contact the operator (from a public phone-box or kindly neighbour) to prompt connection at the exchange.

When the removal van arrives, don't automatically start unpacking the first box which comes off it, even though the van will have been loaded in some kind of order. Instead, have a plan of what to deal with in order of importance, so that you are not worn out from unpacking incidentals, before you get round to unpacking the things you need immediately. The order of unpacking will depend on personal priorities, but most people agree that it is very tedious to find yourself hunting for sheets and bedding late in the evening when you are tired, especially with fractious children who are equally worn out, so it is advisable to make up the beds as a priority.

If the property was furnished and occupied when you viewed it, it might look quite different when empty. You may even be dismayed to find that the room sizes are smaller than they seemed before, or that electric sockets are not suitably positioned to make your usual seat-ing arrangement workable. If this is the case, resist the temptation to spend too much time rearranging the furniture immediately on arrival, which will only lead to irritation and take up valuable unpacking time. Instead it is better to give the matter some thought overnight and then tackle it with a fresh eye the following day.

Storage

If you are involved in a staggered move – you may perhaps be selling your existing home and moving into temporary accommodation before buying again – it will be necessary to put some or all of the furniture and possessions into storage. Many removal companies, especially the larger ones, offer storage facilities as part of their service. The loading and unloading procedures are much the same as for a normal move, but with a gap between them. The removal men arrive to load up in the usual way and then take the cargo to the storage site. Stored goods are sometimes held in warehouses, but nowadays containers are commonly used. The goods are transferred from your home into sealed containers which remain unopened until they are delivered to the final destination. This reduces the chance of loss or damage and also cuts down on dust and dirt.

DID YOU KNOW?   *Some storage companies offer rental of secure individual units. You are given a key to your unit, and have unlimited access.*

You can store virtually everything, except plants, perishable goods, and anything flammable. Special packing is not usually needed to protect goods during a short storage period, although carpets or rugs should ideally be cleaned beforehand and clothes treated against moths.

Deciding which possessions to store needs careful thought. You do not want to omit anything which it later transpires could have been stored, so it is useful to make a comprehensive list of items which are supplied at your temporary accommodation (like bedding or kitchen equipment), so that you know exactly what it would be superfluous to bring yourself. If you find that some items need to be added to your container, the storage company can usually arrange this, as long as you deliver them to the storage site yourself. If you ask nicely and do not make a habit of it, you might not be charged a fee, but check first.

The opposite problem occurs when something is accidentally put into storage. If something needs to be retrieved from the container before the goods are delivered *en masse*, the storage company will almost certainly charge a fee, and will probably need advance notice so that the container can be opened at the company's convenience. If you know you are likely to need some items sooner than the rest, speak to the storage company in advance and it will advise whether or not it can store specific items separately so that they are available for collection on demand. If the company delivers them, there will be a charge.

Using storage facilities could double the cost of moving because everything is moved twice: once into storage containers, then out of storage to the final destination. Storage charges are usually made per container, per week, and as a general guide an average three-bed house or flat will fill around 3 containers.

The storage company will probably prepare its own inventory of furniture and other large items like rugs and appliances, but the precise contents of each box will not be specified, saying only 'carton of books' or 'carton of china'. It is therefore useful to prepare a comprehensive inventory yourself, identifying what is packed into each box, showing for example that box No.1 contains kitchen equipment, so that it can be unloaded straight into the kitchen and not hidden under several other cartons in another room.

As with normal removals, insurance cover for goods under storage is generally on a replacement basis rather than 'new for old'. 'Owner packed' goods are not usually covered by the storage company's insurance for breakage. Your own insurance company might be able to offer better cover, so check with it first before taking out insurance through the storage company.

Kids on the move

The age of your children will probably determine the amount of involvement they have in the move, or whether they are there on the day at all. Very young children might be best left with grandparents or friends, especially if the parents are likely to find the ordeal stressful and relay that to the child. If the children have not participated in the move, bear in mind that on arrival at their new home they could feel rather disorientated, so try to allow for exploration of their new surroundings and time for them to settle in before bedtime. If the children are old enough to understand the move, they will want to get their bearings on arrival at the new home. Once they have satisfied their curiosity, they could be kept busy with drawing or a puzzle in a quiet spot where they can't get into any mischief and won't get under your feet. Letting children select a favourite toy to bring with them, rather than hunting for something suitable amongst packed boxes when you arrive, reduces the chance of tantrums.

Older children generally like to be involved, and would probably enjoy arranging their own bedrooms. If possible, it is helpful for them to see their new home in advance of the move, so that they know what to expect.

When to tell children about a move depends on the individual child and how you think he or she will react to the news. Young children do not understand why they are moving and can become quite distressed when told of an impending change. If they are upset by the idea, enlarge on the positive aspects of the move, like a park or swimming pool nearby, so that they have something nice to look forward to. Older children should really be told about the move early on in proceedings, especially if they need to change schools. Joining a different school as 'the new kid' can be a frightening prospect and may take some getting used to. Telling the child early on also safeguards against the possibility of them finding out by accident from someone else.

As regards schooling, if the move necessitates a change of school you need to contact the local authority covering the area you are moving to, asking them to send information about the schools in that area. You also need to write to the head teacher at the child's current school to advise when he or she is leaving.

If you have children of any age, it is useful to ask the existing occupiers of your new home if there are children of a similar age to yours nearby, so that your offspring can make new friends immediately.

Pets on the move

Pets have no understanding of what is happening to their home when it gets turned upside down on moving day, so making an extra fuss of them will help to allay their fears and confusion. Naturally it is essential to make sure pets have water available at all times and it is a good idea to have at least enough food for the first few days in the new home to tide you over until you have the time and energy to go shopping.

For pets who have identity chip implants, advise the company which holds the register that the contact address has changed.

Cats

Cats have a habit of going AWOL just as the last items are placed in the removal van, so keeping them safely inside avoids a delay while you try to find Tiddles who has decided to disappear for a few hours. A loose cat in the car is a hazard for the driver, so it is preferable to transport them in a suitable container with plenty of ventilation.

On arrival at the new home, cats should be kept inside until they are settled or else you may find that, being territorial animals, they try to find their way back 'home'. The length of time a cat needs to be kept inside depends to some extent on whether he has moved before, and the personality of the individual, but most cats need at least a few days to settle in before confronting their new environment. Have plenty of cat litter and a suitable tray for the period of confinement, and remember to change the address on the identity tag.

TOP TIP

Letting a cat outside for the first time shortly before feeding time, ensures that there is something tempting for him or her come back for.

Dogs

Dogs are usually happier in the garden whilst the loading is under way, assuming it is escape proof, and weather permitting. If a dog is nervous or apt to guard, he will find the presence of removal men something of a worry, and will be far more relaxed away from the proceedings. A good long walk on the morning of the move helps to settle most dogs, and with a bit of luck he will snooze contentedly whilst the packing and loading takes place.

When transporting a dog by car, allow him plenty of ventilation. If travelling a long distance the dog will need regular stops to relieve himself, but it is not advisable, given the strange surroundings and the upset of the move, to let him off the lead.

> **DID YOU KNOW?** *Dogs can die in cars very quickly on a warm day, even if the sun is not shining. They can also suffer heat stroke in a moving car, even in cold weather, when the sun shines on them through the windows, especially in hatch-backs.*

On arrival at the new home, check that fences and boundaries are secure enough to prevent escape if you intend putting a dog in the garden, especially if he is to be left unattended whilst the unpacking gets underway. Put the dog's bed, toys, feeding and water bowls in a suitable place and let him identify them, so that at least something in the new surroundings is normal. If you have rules about which areas of the home your dog has access to, you should establish these as soon as possible to avoid confusion.

Other animals

Small animals such as gerbils and hamsters should be contained in their cage or a suitable box (one which they cannot chew through) and transported with you, *not* in the removals van amongst other boxes and crates. For fish, birds and exotic pets, consult your vet or supplier for specialist advice.

PART TWO
OWNING YOUR HOME

1. HOUSEHOLD SERVICES

Gas

For your own safety, if you have mains gas, it is imperative that you know where the control valve is situated (sometimes in the same box as the meter) so that you can quickly turn off the supply in an emergency. If the meter box is usually locked, make sure you know where the key is at all times. If you have any doubts about how to turn off the gas, ask the supply company to explain it to you. Never ignore the smell of gas. Turn off the supply, open all windows and doors, and report the suspected leak to the gas company (the telephone number will be in the local telephone directory under 'Gas'). Any naked flames, such as pilot lights, should be extinguished, but electrical switches should not be used – so do not turn off any lights or other appliances.

You will be billed for the gas you use every three months, although the bill may estimate how much has been used if the meter has not been read by a representative of the gas company. If the bill is estimated, you will see the letter E alongside the reading. An estimated bill can usually be returned with the actual meter reading (taken by you) so that a more accurate bill can be issued.

Since the gas supply market was deregulated, some areas of the country are now served by gas companies other than British Gas. Switching to a different supply company does not involve the installa-tion of new pipes and meters. The independent gas companies simply rent the pipes and meters which already serve the customer from Transco (British Gas distribution company). They buy the gas itself from the drilling companies, then bill the customer according to the amount of gas used, in the normal way. Currently, the new companies are charging their customers less than British Gas.

Mains gas is not available to every home, and many people who live in rural areas have to buy their gas in cylinders or have it delivered into a storage tank. This type of gas is different from mains gas, and most appliances which have been manufactured to use mains gas are not able to use it, although it is sometimes possible to adapt the appliance, by, for example installing different cooker jets. There are appliances designed specifically for the bottled-gas market, often available through the same agents as sell the fuel.

> **DID YOU KNOW?**   *It is illegal to use a gas appliance if you know or suspect that it might be dangerously faulty, leaking or poorly ventilated.*

Some gas appliances with open flues have been responsible for emitting poisonous carbon monoxide gas. This gas is odourless and colourless, giving no warning of danger, and it can kill. Gas appliances should be used in accordance with the manufacturers' instructions and serviced regularly. Only competent engineers are allowed to install and repair gas appliances – DIYers are not.

> **DID YOU KNOW?**   *You must grant access to an official of the gas supply company in an emergency, or face a fine.*

Electricity

Electricity is supplied via an underground cable, through a meter, then into the home. The electricity company is responsible for the meter itself and any cable going into it from outside. You are responsible for cables and wiring inside the home.

From the supplier's meter (which records the amount of electricity used) the current passes into a consumer-unit containing fused circuits. Different circuits supply power to different outlets, e.g. plugs, light sockets, cooker or shower, and the fuse rating varies depending on the use. You may find that all the lights on the ground floor go out if the relevant fuse blows, but the lights upstairs are unaffected because they are on a different circuit. An electric cooker always has its own circuit.

Meters in modern homes are sometimes housed on the outside of the building, whereas older properties tend to have theirs under the stairs or tucked away in a cupboard in the hall area. A representative from the supply company calls periodically to read the meter for billing purposes, but if he or she cannot gain access to the meter because no one is home, an estimated bill will be issued. If the reading on an estimated bill is inaccurate (which it is likely to be) and you are not happy with the amount charged, it is usually possible to telephone the supplier with more accurate figures and they will then issue a revised bill.

As a safety precaution, many homes, certainly newly built ones, have a modern consumer-unit which contains miniature circuit breakers instead of old-fashioned fuses, and an earth leakage circuit breaker. Often known as a 'trip meter', this device 'trips' (switches off) the supply when there is an earth current leak. For example, if a picture hook or nail is accidentally hammered through a wire in the wall, the current is automatically switched off in a fraction of a second, possibly saving your life.

If one of your fuses blows or a circuit breaker turns the power off, you must find the fault and put it right; you must not simply replace the fuse or reset the circuit breaker. Once you know which appliance is faulty, disconnect it until the fault is rectified.

Some homes are fitted with an additional meter (often called a *white meter*) which separately measures electricity consumed between selected periods of the day. During these hours, for example between midnight and 7 am (times vary to limit the load), electricity used is charged at a lower 'off-peak' tariff. This arrangement is only found in homes which heat their water with electricity and/or have electric heating such as night storage heaters, which use the off-peak power to store heat in insulated blocks, and then gradually release the heat as the blocks cool down during the day.

Treat electricity with respect. It can and does kill. Unlike gas, where the smell gives some warning of a leak, electricity gives no such hint of danger, so it is important to be aware that any electrical appliance has the capacity to give a nasty shock or worse.

- Don't overload sockets with multi-adapters.
- Make sure plugs are wired properly and fitted with the correct fuse.
- Replace worn or damaged flexes or fittings.
- Turn off appliances and unplug when not in use, particularly when retiring to bed.
- Never use electrical appliances near water – for example do not use a portable heater in the bathroom; and always dry your hands before handling an appliance connected to the electricity supply.
- New products should carry the BEAB (British Electrotechnical Approvals Board) mark, which shows they comply with safety tests, so look for this when making any new purchases.
- Be cautious of second-hand appliances. Always check the flex, the plug and the appliance itself for wear or damage before using.

Telephone

Once a telephone line is connected to the property, you can have as many extensions as you like. The wiring needed for an extension line does not need to be purchased through the supplier (line box extension kits are available through many retail outlets), and you can save yourself the cost of an engineer's bill (BT currently charge over £70) if you carry out the simple fitting yourself.

Now that British Telecom no longer has a monopoly on telephone services, you may decide to use one of the other suppliers. Mercury claims to save its subscribers money on long distance and overseas calls. All the subscriber does to divert calls onto the Mercury system is to dial 132 before the normal number. This service is available within 48 hours of contacting the supplier, or alternatively, Mercury supplies a 'LineWise' socket to fit on to the existing BT socket which automatically routes calls through the Mercury system if they are not local. Local calls remain with BT because they are cheaper that way.

> **DID YOU KNOW?** *If your telephone exchange is digital (most now are) you can dial 1471 to find out the telephone number of the last person who called you. You can also dial 5 if a number you are trying to call is engaged – when the person replace the receiver, your handset gives a distinctive ring and reconnects the call automatically. The cost is 10p per ring back.*

A telephone is almost a necessity of 90s living, but it can become a major expense, especially if there are youngsters using it, so some house rules will help to stop the bills spiralling out of control. You might insist that youngsters always ask before using the phone, and restrict calls to a maximum duration of, say, 5 minutes. A timer by the phone is a continuous reminder that time is money. If this doesn't work, you could consider installing a pay phone (not the big public type, but a small domestic one) which means calls are paid for as they are made and you can set the cost of calls. BT sell such a telephone for around £150. You could rent one, but the rental charge at around £42 per quarter plus line rental makes buying more cost-effective in the long run.

You can also organize call barring through the exchange, limiting outgoing calls to 999 and operator service only, or other degrees of call limit. The cost for this service is £7 per quarter, but premium-rate calls can be barred free of charge. If all else fails, a lock might be the only answer.

You can ask for an itemized bill showing the number dialled, the duration of the call and the charge. This lets you see where your money is going and helps identify who used the phone to call whom, when, for how long and at what cost.

As well as the different rates for local and long distance calls, many others exist which are more expensive than usual calls. Telephone numbers with the prefix 0891, for example, usually charge 39p per minute cheap rate and 49p at all other times, which is much more than the standard charges of 5p and 9p per minute respectively. Look out for these numbers and avoid them if possible. The way they work is that the subscriber who takes out a 0891 number receives revenue from calls made to it, which pays for the prize or service offered 'free' to callers. Free phone numbers like 0800 are charged to the subscriber, not the caller.

TAKE A TIP
Avoid calling an 0891 number from a public phone box;
the cost of your call will be more than doubled.

BT's 'cheap rate' applies to calls made between 6 pm and 8 am; daytime rate is 8 am to 6 pm, and weekend calls have a separate rate again. The old 'peak rate' for morning calls has now been abolished. Obviously it is advantageous to make non-essential calls when the cheaper rates apply, especially long social chats.

Cordless phones have become very popular and many people use them as an extension to their normal telephone system. They can be purchased through many retail outlets and do not normally require expert fitting. The equipment is plugged into the telephone socket in the usual way, and is also plugged into the electricity supply so that the battery is charged when not in use. The battery has to be charged regularly, but other static extensions still operate even if the cordless phone's battery is dead.

TAKE A TIP
As a way of avoiding nuisance calls, women should ask to be
listed in the telephone directory by their initials only, omitting
Miss or Mrs.

Mobile telephones offer a completely different service from those using land lines because they work from radio waves. Mobile phone services are available through the many specialist retail outlets which have sprung up over recent years, as well as some electrical stores. Connection is quick and easy. Potential subscribers simply go along to a mobile phone retailer, choose a handset, then complete an application form and direct debit instruction. The retailer then rings the supplier for authorization and a credit check, and if all is well you are allocated a number for incoming calls and are connected to the network there and then. You usually have to enter into a contract with the supplier for a minimum of 12 months, after which termination of the service is possible by giving the required amount of notice. A regular subscription charge is payable whether or not you make any calls. Handsets are purchased rather than rented and they vary greatly in price and quality, so look out for special offers. Many are virtually given away to encourage custom. The handsets are powered by a battery which is recharged by plugging it into the mains. Different handsets give different lengths of usage on a single charge, and some are better than others in this respect.

Invaluable as the telephone is, it can sometimes be pose a security risk. As a precaution, women and children should never tell callers whom they do not know and trust that they are alone. If a caller asks to speak to someone unknown to you, do not volunteer your name or telephone number, and certainly not your address. Instead, ask what number the caller dialled. If the number is not yours, tell the caller he has misdialled. If the number dialled is yours, tell the caller he has been given the wrong number.

Nuisance and obscene calls are relatively rare but can be very upsetting. It is important to keep calm and not to give the caller the response he is looking for. Don't enter into a conversation and, difficult though it is, try not to give the impression that you are distressed or angry. Even slamming the phone down can be enough incentive for the caller to ring again, so instead, place the handset by the phone then carry on with whatever you were doing for a few minutes (you could unplug at the wall so that the caller cannot hear you moving around), then calmly replace the receiver without checking to see if the caller is still there. The caller will probably withhold his number, but if not (he may be stupid as well as a nuisance) it could be retrieved by dialling 1471. Make a note of it and report the incident to the police.

If the phone rings immediately after a nuisance call and you decide to answer it, do not speak first. If the caller is not genuine he will probably just hang up. If you prefer not to answer the phone when it next rings, leave it, then dial 1471, and if the recorded number is one you recognize, you can call it back.

BT have a helpline on 0800 666700, where you can get advice from a recorded message. If the problem is serious, BT can work with the police to trace the calls – obscene and indecent calls are a criminal offence and the perpetrators can be prosecuted. You can have your existing telephone number changed, and you might consider having the new number excluded from the directory.

Water

Your water supply enters the property from the main service pipe and then divides, going direct to the kitchen sink on the one hand and to the cold water tank on the other. From the tank (usually situated in the loft), the water falls by gravity into various taps, the WC cistern and the hot water cylinder. It is important to know where the stop valves are. If you need to turn off the water in an emergency or for maintenance, you do not want to be hunting around whilst the flood waters rise and the plumber adds the delay to his bill. The internal stop valve is often under the kitchen sink, and there will also be one outside the property which the water company can access if necessary.

Most homes have a cold water tank and a hot water tank. However, if you have a combination boiler which heats water as it is used, instead of storing hot water in bulk, you do not have a hot water tank, and possibly no cold water tank either. This system is cost-effective for small households because it only heats water on demand.

If you use a sprinkler to water the garden, you will probably have to pay an annual charge. If a drought order is imposed during a period of excessively dry weather, the use of sprinklers and hose-pipes is routinely banned. If you ignore this ban, you could find yourself in hot water!

> **DID YOU KNOW?** *If your property is unoccupied and unfurnished, you may not have to pay water charges.*

The water company takes responsibility for repairing the mains supply pipes which are outside your property boundary. If the supply pipes within your boundary spring a leak, you will be responsible for the repair costs.

All water companies must meet certain standards of service, and a list of these can be obtained by contacting the relevant company. Some companies voluntarily exceed minimum standards by offering larger compensation amounts to customers if they fail to meet their own standards, and by attempting to further reduce delays in restoring supplies and answering customer queries.

Burst pipes and flooding

Given that large quantities of water criss-cross the home, supplying taps, WC etc., it is no wonder that occasionally a pipe might spring a leak or burst. It might be possible to repair a leaking pipe temporarily by bandaging it with suitable adhesive tape. Although insulating pipes will help to protect them from severe weather, occasionally a pipe may get cold enough for the water in it to freeze. Pipes burst when they freeze, not when they thaw, so if you can detect a rupture in a frozen pipe you can repair it before water starts to leak as it thaws. You will need to turn off the water supply at the mains and then empty water out of the system quickly by leaving the taps on, so that the water goes down the drain and not down the walls! Then you can start to thaw out the (repaired) pipe, working from the outlet end first, either by using a hairdryer, or by applying dry towels around the pipe and then pouring hot water over them. Do not use an electric fire underneath a frozen pipe.

If a rising main bursts, turn off the supply then call a plumber. If you notice water outside the property seeping or gushing through the ground, call the water supplier.

A serious flood in the loft is rare, but if you are unlucky enough to experience one you will need to act quickly by puncturing the ceiling below in several places in order to prevent the whole ceiling coming down under the weight of water. Buckets placed under the puncture points will catch some of the water, but if the flood is serious you can expect some secondary flooding underneath. Turn off the supply and empty the system by leaving the kitchen tap on, then call a plumber.

Refuse collection

Household refuse is usually collected weekly. Some areas enjoy a flexible service which includes collection of almost anything, including garden trimmings, whilst others find that anything not put into refuse sacks is left behind. For disposal of rubbish which is not collected, contact the local council to find out where the nearest tip is located. The charge for refuse collection is included in the Council Tax.

Council Tax

The Council Tax was introduced in 1993 and is a combination of personal and property tax, payable to the local council with responsibility for collection. The funds are a contribution to the cost of providing services such as housing, leisure facilities and car parks, education, the fire brigade, libraries and magistrates courts, and the police force. Council Tax payments cover only part of the cost of providing these services, the majority of funds come from Government grants.

The amount of your Council Tax bill is based on the value of your home. The local valuation office (part of the Inland Revenue in England and Wales but independent in Scotland) assesses the value of each dwelling based on its estimated selling value at 1 April 1991. Each home falls into one of eight 'bands' according to its market value:

England:

Band A	Up to £40,000
Band B.	£40,001– £52,000
Band C	£52,001–£68,000
Band D	£68,001–£88,000
Band E	£88,001–£120,000
Band F	£120,001–£160,000
Band G	£160,001–£320,000
Band H	Over £320,000

Wales:

Band A	Under £30,000
Band B	£30,001– £39,000
Band C	£39,001– £51,000
Band D	£51,001–£66,000
Band E	£66,001–£90,000
Band F	£90,001–£120,000
Band G	£120,001–£240,000
Band H	Over £240,000

Scotland:

Band A	Up to £27,000
Band B	£27,001– £35,000
Band C	£35,001–£45,000
Band D	£45,001–£58,000
Band E	£58,001–£80,000
Band F	£80,001–£106,000
Band G	£106,001–£212,000
Band H	Over £212,000

There are some exceptions and reductions. Buildings are exempt from Council Tax if, for example, they are unoccupied and unfurnished, owned by a charity, occupied solely by students or unfit for habitation. The banding assumes that the dwelling is occupied by two adults over 18 years old. If more than two adults live in the dwelling the bill is not increased, but if only one adult is the occupier, he or she may qualify for a 25% discount. If all those resident in a dwelling are exempt from paying the personal proportion of the Council Tax the bill could be reduced by 50%.

Although people receiving Income Support are liable to pay Council Tax, if their circumstances are such that there is no other income coming into the home, they usually receive a 100% rebate. It is important to realize that relief is not automatic and there is a liability to pay until the appropriate forms have been completed and approved by the collector. Families on a low income may qualify for Council Tax benefit.

> **DID YOU KNOW?**   *If the home you buy has been significantly improved since it was valued for Council Tax purposes, the tax banding may be raised when it is sold to you.*

The valuation that is used to arrive at the market value of each home (and subsequently its banding) is not always accurate, and could be wrong as a result of inconclusive or incorrect observations. If you have reason to believe your banding is incorrect, you can appeal against it, but a decrease in market values since the original valuation is not reason enough for an alteration to the valuation list. However, if the property has suffered a significant reduction in value since it was valued – perhaps part of it has been demolished – or if the value has been reduced because of a new road or other nearby redevelopment, then there could be an argument for reducing the banding. While the appeal is in progress, you must still pay the bill until the appeal is settled. If the appeal is granted in your favour, a refund will be arranged accordingly.

At the beginning of the financial year (1 April), you will be sent a Council Tax bill for the year to 31 March following, showing the annual amount due. The bill can be paid in instalments, either using a payment book or by completing a direct debit mandate form.

Punishment for non-payment of the Council Tax can be severe.

2. HOUSEHOLD BILLS

Most suppliers give their customers plenty of payment options, and many of them are happy to accept payment by instalment, either as a way of spreading the cost of one-off annual bills such as those for a TV licence or insurance premiums, or as a steady contribution towards future bills. Instalments are usually paid by direct debit or standing order arrangements (see below).

If you prefer to pay your bills as they arrive, you can do so by sending a cheque or postal order with the relevant payment slip. Sending cash is not advisable, but if you have no alternative, use registered post. Alternatively, many bills can be paid through banks by presenting the payment slip and payment, but expect a fee if using a bank where you do not have an account. Post offices also accept payment of bills. Usually there is no counter charge, but if there is, the bill will say so.

Standing orders and direct debits

Standing orders and direct debits are both ways of paying bills through a bank or building society account. A standing order is an instruction for the bank to pay the payee a set amount at specified intervals, such as monthly or quarterly. A direct debit is written authority for the bank to release funds on demand of the payee, the amounts of which can be variable. A standing order might therefore be used to make a regular charity donation, whereas a direct debit is more suitable for mortgage repayments because the repayment amount may alter every now and then. If a standing order were used, it would have to be formally amended each time the repayment amount changed, which is a nuisance to the borrower and an administrative nightmare for the lender, and any resulting delay would throw the payment pattern off course.

Many suppliers of services accept payment by direct debit, and arranging this is simply a matter of completing a form from the supplier, giving details of the bank or building society and the account number. This form then authorizes your bank to make the required payment, without your having to bother with writing out cheques or remembering to send them on time.

> **DID YOU KNOW?**   *Some suppliers offer a discount to customers who pay by direct debit.*

You can pay most bills by direct debit or standing order, including insurance (buildings, contents and vehicle), TV licence, gas, electricity, telephone, water and community charge.

Budget plans

This type of arrangement allows you to make payments towards a bill before it becomes due. The benefit is that you will not suddenly receive a large bill for which you have not made provision.

Budget accounts or budget payment plans work by estimating how much your bill will amount to over the following year, then dividing that sum by twelve to calculate equal monthly payments. If, at the end of the year, your account is in credit or debit, you will be given a refund or asked to make up the difference to brings the account back to zero. If the credit or debit amount is substantial, the monthly payment for the next year may be altered in an effort to avoid this happening again. Payments are usually made by direct debit or standing order.

Savings stamps

This system is a way of putting money aside for payment of an anticipated bill. The stamps are sold in set denominations available from the supplier, and then used to pay the bill when it arrives.

Meters

Electricity and gas can be paid for as it is used if a meter is installed, but the unit costs may be higher. The meter is usually fed with a card or tokens purchased from the supplier. Sometimes a supplier may insist that the customer uses a meter, if there is reason to doubt that bills would be settled.

Payment protection schemes

Payment protection plans come in various forms, but the object of them all is to offer insurance against the inability to meet a financial commitment, whether that might be making mortgage repayments or paying the gas bill. In most cases, a monthly premium payment is made to an insurance company, in return for which the insurance company agrees to make payments (the amount of which depends on the amount of cover) in the event of a claim. As with any insurance, there are exclusions in the policy, so it is vital to be aware of these before taking out the cover, to make sure it is worth having.

Payment difficulties

If there is little leeway between income and outgoings, the latter can easily become the greater figure, resulting in quite sudden debt. It is an over-simplification to say that someone heading towards debt should see it coming and do something about it before it happens. In reality, a tight budget can topple into a financial crisis overnight.

Most suppliers of essential services understand this and are happy to help their customers over a difficult period without much fuss, as long as you show that you intend to pay the bill, and are not simply refusing to pay it. But if customers do not approach them, how are they to know the difference? All the supplier sees is an unpaid bill, and with no knowledge of the individual's circumstances the wheels of debt-recovery and withdrawal of services are set in motion. This is one of the reasons why it is so important to approach the supplier as soon as you face payment difficulties. Don't wait for a temporary cash-flow problem to get out of hand before asking for help. If you cannot pay a bill, either because you were not expecting it to be so high or because your income has been reduced (see below for information on state benefits), tell the supplier immediately, preferably before the bill arrives.

Companies who supply public utilities, such as gas and electricity, will cut off the service to a customer if you do not pay your bills, but only if all other avenues have been exhausted. Customers must be given clear written warning of the intention to withdraw the service (7 days' notice for gas, 21 days' notice for electricity), after which an official will call to cut off the supply. If you do not allow the official entry into your home, which is your right, then an entry warrant will be applied for through the magistrates' court. When the official returns with the warrant, you must allow him access, or face a fine. However, if you arrange to pay off the debt by reasonable instalments before the situation gets to this stage, the company will usually reconsider.

If the supply is cut off, the company can demand a deposit before they will reconnect you, although this is not usually charged if you have arranged to settle your debt by instalment.

Gas will not be cut off in the winter (between October and March), as long as everyone in the home who has an income receives a state retirement pension. Also, it will not be cut off if the debt relates to a previous customer, i.e. the person who lived in the property before, provided you made proper arrangements to take over the supply before you moved in. If you receive a bill which you think is incorrect, you can usually withhold that part which you consider is excessive, as long as you explain to the supplier what you are doing, and pay the rest of the bill.

It is perhaps naïve to expect all creditors to be sympathetic to tales of woe, and they will sometimes feel justified in recovering money owed by whatever means open to them. However, in most cases if you offer to make instalment payments of a reasonable amount to repay the debt over a reasonable length of time, this is usually enough to keep the matter out of court.

Keeping fuel bills down

Avoiding wastage

Wasting fuel is a terrible waste of money. As consumers we often go to the trouble of saving a few pence on the shopping bill by buying in bulk, using own-brand goods or travelling to out-of-town supermarkets, yet our fuel bills are higher than they need to be because so much of it is wasted. Take a look at your heating arrangements, and see if you can make any savings.

- A room which is rarely used, a guest bedroom for example, needs little or no heating when not occupied.
- Some rooms need less heating than others. If you heat your kitchen but often open the window because cooking makes the room too hot, this is a prime example of wastage.
- Your home does not need to be heated when no one is at home, e.g. in the middle of the day when everyone is out at work or school.
- Experiment with room temperatures – you may find you can lower your thermostat setting by a few degrees and not notice the difference.
- Do you really need the central heating on overnight?
- Do you heat more water than you need?
- Do you leave lights on in unoccupied rooms?

TAKE A TIP
Supplies of solid fuel like coal and oil can often be purchased more cheaply during the summer months and stored until needed.

The kitchen offers many fuel-saving opportunities:
- On cookers, match saucepan and ring sizes.
- Keep saucepan lids on whenever possible, or use a metal plate to keep the heat in.
- Cook as many things together as you can. If heating the oven for one item, try to cook the whole meal in it at the same time, rather than cooking the pudding after the main course for example. More than one vegetable can be cooked in the same pan – you can even buy pans with separate compartments for this.
- Using the grill to cook, say, a lamb chop, is cheaper than using the oven, but for toast a toaster is more economical than the grill.
- Boil water in a kettle rather than saucepan, and boil only as much as you need.

TAKE A TIP

If you have off-peak electricity, you could reduce your
electricity bill by using some appliances (dishwasher, washing
machine, tumble dryer) late at night or early in the morning,
to take advantage of the reduced tariff. Beware, however,
that running appliances overnight when the household sleeps
is a potential fire risk.

Using insulation

Good insulation not only makes life more comfortable, it also significantly
reduces heating bills. Poor insulation allows heat to escape from the
building and also means that you are continually having to heat cold air
as it comes through gaps in windows and doors.

• Loft insulation

Loft insulation is relatively easy and quick to install. Glass fibre wadding
is supplied in rolls which fit between the joists. If installing your own,
remember that this material is an irritant, so wear gloves and a face mask
when handling it. Most homes have some loft insulation, but unless it is
at least 4″ thick, the full benefit probably won't be felt.

TAKE A TIP

Insulating the loft keeps heat in the rooms below but makes
consequently makes the loft area colder. Because of this, the
cold water tank (and pipes) may need to be lagged to prevent
them freezing in the winter. You can help to avoid freezing in
the loft by leaving the hatch open a few inches in particularly
cold weather.

• Cavity wall insulation

Most modern homes have either partial cavity insulation, which leaves an
air gap between the insulation boards and the outer walls, or full

insulation which completely fills the area between the inner and outer walls. The insulating benefits of this are obvious, so if you do not have cavity insulation it might be a worthwhile investment for comfort, and as a way of cutting fuel bills. The cavity between the inner and outer walls is injected with either foam or mineral fibre through small holes drilled in the outer wall. Because the work is done outside the property, there is no need to have workmen traipsing through your home with machinery and dirty boots, and the job only takes a day or two for the average property. Strict safety standards apply, so make sure the installer adheres to these. Foam products must conform to British Standard 5617 and the installation method to British Standard 5618. Installers of mineral fibre must have an Agrément Board certificate for the material and installation method.

Properties which are subjected to extreme weather conditions in winter might not be suitable candidates for this type of insulation, so always get expert advice before going ahead. Also, injected insulating materials should not be used for properties of timber frame construction, or for those which already have partial cavity insulation.

• Lagging water tanks
Hot water tanks should be lagged with a 3″ thick padded lagging jacket, otherwise the water temperature will drop very quickly. A lagging jacket is not expensive, is easy to fit, and will probably pay for itself in a few months. Modern hot water tanks are often factory-lagged with fitted insulation.

• Eliminating draughts
Draughty doors and window frames not only allow heat to escape, but also bring cold air into the room. If you do not have double glazing and are losing a lot of heat through old or draughty windows, you could consider having secondary glazing fitted. This 'second window', fitted across the inside of the existing frame, provides an air gap between inner and outer window panes, so as well as reducing heat loss can also help with condensation problems (and provide some sound-insulation).

Whilst secondary glazing can be rather unsightly, it is usually cheaper than replacing the whole window, especially if the replacement window would need to be custom made.

As an instant cure for draughts, try one of the many draught excluders on the market. For windows, adhesive strips work well and can be installed in minutes. The same type of strip can be used around the inside of door frames to ensure a snug fit between door and frame, and a draught excluder fitted onto the bottom of the door is simple to fit and costs very little.

Heavy curtains, especially if they are lined or have a thermal backing, offer good insulation, but if they hang over a radiator most of the heat will go straight up the back of the curtains.

When eliminating draughts, remember that heating appliances need suitable and adequate ventilation for safe operation. For example, the type of gas appliance which imitates a coal fire may need a ventilation grille fitted in the room, depending on the amount of fuel it burns. This is because the fire needs air to operate and takes this from the room. If the fire cannot get enough air, the flame burns incorrectly, resulting in the emission of carbon monoxide gas.

Solid floors are often cold, and this is a big problem to rectify. Raising the floor level on timber joists and laying insulating material underneath is a solution, but an expensive one. Thick carpet will help, or alternatively you could consider replacing the existing underlay with a thicker version, although a good quality underlay can be almost as expensive as new carpet, so cost out the project carefully.

3. REPAIRS AND MAINTENANCE

Owning a property is an expensive business, and anyone considering it should be fully aware of the huge financial commitment involved. It is not just the steady stream of bills for gas, electricity, telephone, etc. which cause a financial drain (you would have those whatever your living arrangements), but that the cost of keeping a property in reasonable condition is an ongoing expense. You cannot own a property and ignore routine maintenance. If you do, minor maintenance jobs soon escalate into major repairs. Never is the saying 'a stitch in time saves nine' more apt than when applied to property maintenance.

If the prospect of continually maintaining a property worries you, buying a leasehold might be less of a strain than taking on a freehold. Lessees contribute to repairs and maintenance costs as detailed in the lease, but do not generally take direct responsibility for organizing the work, and do not face unexpectedly large bills if maintenance charges are the same amount every year, although these can be high.

> **DID YOU KNOW?** *Some essential repairs may need to be done between exchange of contracts and completion to satisfy your lenders.*

Essential repairs, those which affect the fabric of the building, need to be dealt with promptly, otherwise the property can quickly deteriorate and decrease in value. On this basis, the first things to tackle when taking ownership of your new home are any repairs which, left unattended, could lead to further damage. Water is the enemy of any building, so if you have problems with water penetration they need to be corrected as a priority. There is no point spending a lot of time and money decorating, only to have damp-stains ruin your efforts.

| **TAKE A TIP** |
| When getting quotes for repairs, ask how much disruption will be involved and clarify exactly how long the job will take. |

Some repairs will obviously be more expensive than others, so if you cannot afford to have everything done immediately, you will have to prioritize. Big, expensive jobs do not necessarily take precedence. Small repairs can be just as important to the health of the building. A dislodged gutter is not a big job, but leaving it could cause damage, whereas replacing old fencing is an expensive job which could probably wait.

Basic maintenance – outside

- Gutters and drains should be kept clear of leaves and other debris. A blocked gutter or downpipe can soon lead to water penetration.
- Check the roof regularly for missing/broken tiles or slates, and damaged flashing. Preferably use a proper roof ladder if you intend doing the work yourself, but in any case use one that extends several rungs above the guttering. Work in dry weather. Flat roofs may look safe to stand on, but are not designed to take much weight and the surface material is easily damaged. Damaged asphalt roofs need to be repaired urgently, before the asphalt starts to lift. Whilst checking the roof of the house, take a look also at those on the garage and garden shed.
- Check windows and doors. Woodwork which has been painted or stained needs new coats periodically to protect the wood. If the paint is chipped or flaked, the wood underneath is taking the full force of the weather. Wet rot is a fungus which attacks damp wood. If the wood under flaking paint has darkened in colour and feels soft to the touch, you could have a wet-rot problem. Check that the putty around window panes is providing adequate waterproofing and is not loose or missing altogether, and that the frames have not shrunk away from the masonry. For ledged windows, check the groove underneath the ledge (the drip groove) has not been filled in with

paint. This groove allows water to drip off before it reaches the point at which the ledge attaches to the wall.

TAKE A TIP

Wooden windows which stick could be the result of hinges working loose. Tightening the screws may bring the window back into line and cure the problem.

- Check exterior walls for cracked rendering and/or to see if the brickwork needs repointing. Make sure the damp-proof course is not covered with rubble or soil etc. which make a bridge for moisture to rise over the course, and ensure air bricks are not blocked. If you find efflorescence (a white deposit of salt) on exterior walls, most commonly on newly built homes, brush it away with a dry wire brush. The condition arises when bricks dry out, so do not be tempted to wash it off as this just makes the problem worse. On external walls, efflorescence is not a problem although it is rather unsightly.
- Garden walls and gates, although probably not a priority, should be checked to make sure they are safe and not a hazard to you or anyone else who may call at the property.
- Holes in asphalt driveways need prompt repair to stop the damage spreading.

Basic maintenance – inside

- Look out for signs of damp (mould, damaged timber, musty smells) and find the cause as soon as possible. Often you do not need to be an expert to see quite clearly the source of the problem. By closely inspecting the outside of the building you may find, for example, that part of the rendering has cracked and is letting in rainwater. A condition like this can cause major damage if left unrepaired. On woodwork dry rot may appear. Though less common than wet rot, dry rot is often more difficult to treat and can spread if not eradicated completely. It is usually a result of rising damp or leaking pipes and most commonly appears inside the home in an unventilated area.

169

- Check the loft regularly. By the time you notice a damp patch on the ceiling of the room below, there will be damage in the loft area. The problem might not be from rain penetration, so check pipe-work for leaks as well.
- Condensation can be a real problem in rooms which are not well ventilated, most commonly the kitchen and bathroom. Condensation occurs when warm, damp air, such as steam from cooking or a shower, comes into contact with a cold surface, such as the glass of a window. As well as being unsightly, the resulting moisture of condensation plays havoc with decoration, often causing mould. It may be possible to stop condensation by installing some form of ventilation, like an extractor fan or the type of cooker hood which takes steam out of the room by venting it outside.

TAKE A TIP
To reduce condensation resulting from steam in the bathroom, run some cold water into the bath first, then use a shower attachment or similar to run the hot water in under the cold.

- Chimneys need to be swept regularly to help avoid the risk of the sooty deposits catching fire. Often the first indication of a chimney fire is the noise it makes.
- The boiler and heating system should be regularly serviced to ensure they are in good working order.

Plumbing and heating
- It is important that boilers and water heaters are regularly serviced. Choose a CORGI or Institute of Plumbing registered installer to do the work.
- Make sure you know where services like water, electricity and gas, and also your oil supply, enter your property. You may need to turn them off quickly in an emergency.

- Stopcocks and valves can become seized if they are never used, so it is a good idea to turn them occasionally.
- Make sure that your storage tanks and the expansion tank for your heating system are well insulated and have a suitable cover fitted to stop debris falling into the water.
- Check that ball valves are working correctly and not causing water from the cistern to run through the overflow pipe.
- Do not leave taps dripping for too long before fitting new washers as this will damage tap sealings.
- Periodically check manholes and drains to make sure they have no obstructions. Also check waste traps and waste pipes by removing access covers.
- Check radiators for air.
- Gas appliances have air vents fitted for correct operation, so make sure these are not obstructed internally or externally (by trees, for example). The air supply is an important factor for the correct burning and cooling of an appliance.
- Flues of appliances can be visually checked for obstructions.
- Consider installing a carbon monoxide detector if you use open-flue gas appliances.

Doing it yourself

Most towns have their fair share of DIY superstores, supplying the keen amateur with everything necessary to repair and improve the home. A huge array of DIY products is available, from paint and paper to electrical and plumbing equipment. There seems no limit to the confidence the manufacturers of these products have in the ability of the DIY enthusiast. Unfortunately, whilst the products encourage enthusiasm, they do not instil knowledge, and the accompanying instructions can be deceptively simple.

There are many books available to guide the amateur workman (or woman), but whilst these are informative they cannot give the reader the necessary experience to do the job easily or properly. You may need to do a job more than once before you get it right. This is fine with something like wallpapering – if you are not satisfied with the finish you can always strip it off and start again, which, although tiresome and a waste of paper, is not too much of a problem. Try your hand at something more serious, however, like building work, and you could find yourself facing more than the irritation of wasted time, and end up paying a larger bill to correct your mistakes than it would have cost to employ a professional to do the job in the first place.

Doing jobs yourself can save a lot of money and be very rewarding, but learning a new skill takes practice, and you could find in retrospect that your sitting-room wall is not the best place to practise the art of plastering. The key to successful DIY is to know your limitations; not only limitations of knowledge, but also of time and patience. On the plus side, if you are capable of doing a job yourself, you will probably do it better than any paid contractor, at a fraction of the cost.

Employing contractors

Bad workmanship can lessen the value of your home, so it is essential that the contractors you employ are competent.

Finding a contractor can leave you spoilt for choice, especially if you live in a large town or city where there are hundreds to choose from. The best advertisement for any contractor is personal recommendation, so if friends or neighbours have used a particular firm and been pleased with their work, you could invite this firm to submit a quote. Do not assume, however, that one recommendation is absolute proof of their competence (make sure you are happy to employ them regardless), or of their value, so get other quotes as well.

If you cannot find a contractor through personal recommendation, you may have no other option than to look through the local newspaper or trade directory, but this method of selection is a bit of a lucky dip since you cannot possibly tell how good a contractor is by their advertising style. The Yellow Pages or local newspaper only show those companies who pay to advertise there, so you do not get a full picture of the range of companies available. Also, do not assume that the biggest advertisements represent the biggest (or best) companies. Some small companies go to the expense of paying for large advertisements, whilst companies which are well known don't bother because their reputation speaks for itself. If you do rely on advertisements, look for craftsmen who belong to governing bodies like the Federation of Master Builders and the Institute of Plumbing, which only grant membership to companies who work to a certain standard. This membership is not an absolute guarantee that the work will be good, but if a contractor does not belong to an appropriate governing body perhaps you should ask why not before employing him.

DID YOU KNOW? *Companies who install or service gas appliances must be registered with CORGI (The Council for Registered Gas Installers). Before instructing work, ask your intended installer for his registration number and check it with CORGI (tel: 01256 708133).*

Some companies reproduce written references from 'satisfied customers' in their promotional literature, and whilst these references may be genuine, there could be just as many customers who are dissatisfied, so take them with a pinch of salt. If you can, ask to see examples of previous work for yourself.

Always obtain quotes from several different companies and make sure the cheapest ones include as much work as the more expensive ones before assuming you have found a bargain. You will almost certainly find variations between contractors. Ask for a written quotation showing the full amount you will be charged, rather than an estimate, which might be altered (upwards usually) when the final bill arrives. If you are having more than one job done, it may be cost effective to spread your custom. If you get a good feeling about a particular contractor, but his quote is high, you could tell him that his prices are not competitive and see if he will bring them into line with other quotes you have received.

Interview each contractor for personal appeal. Would you feel happy to have this person in your home? Will you be able to communicate with him or her? If the answer is no, any problems which arise will be difficult to resolve between you. It is possible to get some idea from meeting a contractor of whether they will do a good job, so trust your instincts. If a contractor calls to survey the work before submitting a quote and you dislike his attitude, don't employ him. If he turns up late, or you have to wait a long time for the quote to arrive, you can reasonably assume that his standard of work will be equally sloppy.

As each contractor calls to prepare a quote, ask what work is involved so that you gain knowledge yourself. After several plumbers have each explained what is needed to install a new bathroom, for example, you will know the system inside out. By the time the last contractor calls to give a quote, you'll be telling him what is involved.

TAKE A TIP

If you intend to employ a contractor to do more than one job, instruct him initially to do just one. If the service and workmanship is good, you can then give him the other work. Tell him what you are doing – he might not like it, but will be in no doubt that further work only follows complete satisfaction.

Never employ friends or family unless they are properly qualified. A friend who has done a lot of work around his own home may have the confidence and kindness to offer to do work for you, and this cheap way of getting a job done may seem very attractive, but it is a potential disaster and you could loose a friend as well as a lot of money if it all goes horribly wrong.

When you have chosen your contractor, and confirmed the price of the job with him (in writing as a quotation), tie him down to a definite starting and finishing date. You do not want to pull out your old kitchen units ready for new ones to be fitted, or pile up your furniture into another room ready for carpet fitting, only to find that the kitchen or carpet will not be fitted for another fortnight.

If the company supplies a contract, setting out the nature of work, payment terms etc., read it carefully and query anything you do not understand or agree with. If it does not prepare a contract, you could do so yourself, reaffirming what you expect from the job.

Don't pay for a job until you have checked the standard of work, seen that everything is in good working order and been given relevant guarantees. You may have to pay a small premium to have insurance-backed guarantee cover on the work, but the cost could be well worth it if the work is unsatisfactory or the company goes out of business. If you are asked to pay for materials before work begins (this is sometimes a fair and legitimate request), get a receipt.

Contractors should have public liability insurance and professional indemnity insurance. If a contractor causes damage whilst working for you, this insurance will be important. If he is not insured, you will have to claim from him personally. You may get away with holding back part of his bill in payment for the damage caused, or until the damage has been rectified, but to avoid the risk of a judgement against you for non-payment, it might be better to pay the bill under protest (written protest), then claim for the damage.

TAKE A TIP
Cover carpets to protect them when contractors are around. In the event of an insurance claim, the ruling may be that damage caused by contractors coming and going with dirty boots is fair wear and tear, refuting a claim for cleaning costs, let alone replacement.

Having decided what work to have done first, and who is going to do it, allow the contractors to get on with the job without interruption, but keep an eye on them. If they know their work is being overseen, they will generally take more care over it and be less inclined to make a mess or cause unnecessary damage.

TAKE A TIP
If your home is clean and tidy, contractors are usually careful to keep it that way. If it is already in a mess, they don't bother too much about adding to this.

---

4. ADDITIONS AND IMPROVEMENTS

Once you move into your new home, you may be tempted to dust off the toolkit immediately and start making all sorts of improvements. This is natural enough as a way of putting your own 'stamp' on a property and make it into a home. However, before investing in major improvements or alterations, consider whether they will add to the value of your home. It makes sense to undertake only those projects which will recoup their cost later, especially if you think you may be selling the property in the not-too-distant future. Of course, if you do not envisage ever leaving your home, then whether a project is cost effective or not will be of little importance: something which brings you pleasure will be reason enough for the financial outlay.

Whether or not a project is cost effective depends primarily on the property's maximum attainable value. If it has the potential to increase in value, i.e. if comparable properties in better condition command a higher price, then money spent on bringing the property up to a good standard will almost certainly be recouped when it is sold.

It is very difficult to categorize those things which you probably will get your money back on, and those which you won't, but generally speaking any custom-made luxury is unlikely to be worth the outlay, whilst 'impact improvements' like internal or external 'face lifts' usually recoup their cost and make a property easier to sell should the need arise.

Extensions can have mixed appeal to future buyers. Take for example a terraced property with a small back garden, extended at the rear to enlarge the kitchen. The extension may be a plus point for buyers wanting more room than the other houses in the terrace offer, but it could dissuade others because the garden has been diminished. If the extension is not in keeping with the rest of the building, of if the build standard is not up to scratch, this could also be detrimental.

> **DID YOU KNOW?** *Some internal walls are load-bearing and should not be removed or altered by, for example, inserting a new doorway. If in doubt get professional advice.*

Your mortgage deed may stipulate that alterations or improvements must have the consent of the lender before work commences. A letter to your lender, setting out the intended work, is usually all that is required. Lenders generally give consent willingly, having no objection to the value of their security being increased.

If you plan to undertake several improvements or alterations, decide on the best order in which to tackle them. If you cannot afford to have everything done immediately, you may have to choose whether to splash out on a big project or to split the available funds between several less expensive ones. Bear in mind that some work inevitably leads to redecoration, so if you intend to extend your lounge, there is not much point decorating it beforehand.

If you intend to do the work yourself, accept your limitations. This doesn't mean that you shouldn't try your hand at a new skill, but remember that undoing a disaster will take much longer and be more expensive than having the job done professionally in the first place. If you intend to employ contractors, refer to the last chapter for some pointers on how to choose them and what to look out for.

There are far too many possible additions or improvements to mention them all, but here are some of the more common ones.

Internal decorating

Internal decoration does not need to cost a fortune. Assuming the condition of the property is sound, i.e. the walls and woodwork are in good condition, and that basic maintenance has not been badly neglected (if so, this should be put right first), a new coat of paint can vastly improve a room, or indeed the whole property, for very little cost. Dark rooms in particular can be transformed with light coloured paint. There are plenty of different colours to choose from, and specific shades can be mixed to order. You do not need to be a decorating expert to use paint. A reasonably steady hand, a step ladder and a few brushes is all you need, and if you don't like the finished result, you can try again with a different colour.

Some paint manufacturers produce small sample pots, so you can try a patch of a likely colour of paint (several, if necessary) before buying a large tin. This is often safer than gauging how a colour will look from shade cards because the printing does not always accurately reproduce the colour, and the finished result will depend on what existing colour you are covering, and whether the room gets light from the north or the south.

TAKE A TIP
If covering an existing colour (especially patterned wallpaper), use an undercoat before applying your chosen colour. This gives a better result, and is less expensive than using several coats of coloured paint.

If the walls are papered, you will probably find it easier to paint over the existing paper rather than take it off, assuming the texture and finish are suitable. However, the person who hung the paper in the first place will need to have done a good job for the finished result to be acceptable. Any peeling corners will need to be stuck down (you can use border adhesive for this) before painting. Applying paint is quick and easy, but stripping wallpaper is both labour intensive and time consuming. Also, the state of the walls underneath the paper might not be quite what it had appeared, and their condition could be the very reason they were covered in the first place. If you do decide to strip, and a poor wall is exposed, this will need to be either replastered or papered again. Whilst some people find hanging wallpaper quicker than painting, the cost is usually higher, so painting over the existing paper is also a cheaper option.

External decorating

Unless the property is single-storey, external decorating involves the use of ladders and/or scaffolding. You may therefore not be able to do the work yourself, and will incur the cost of employing someone to do the job as well as the cost of materials. Properties which have not been rendered, stone-washed or otherwise painted have minimal redecorating requirements, just the windows and doors, but the fashion for painting the outside walls of buildings has left many homeowners with the recurring expense of repainting every so often.

The weather causes problems and delays for external painting. Rain stops work instantly and can be disastrous if it suddenly pours onto a newly glossed window or door. Very hot weather can stop paint drying properly, and in cold weather the decorator might not turn up! Bearing this in mind, it might be worth taking note of the long-range weather forecast before engaging a decorator, and aim to have the work done during a period of warm, dry weather.

Improved heating

Nowadays we tend to live and work in warm, centrally heated environments, so anything less than about 18°C feels decidedly chilly. If your new home is poorly heated you could either upgrade the existing system with better equipment, adding to what is already there, or start again with a completely new system.

If you are not competent to install the heating yourself (and unless you are qualified in this field it would be unwise to try, and incidentally it is illegal for an amateur to install gas appliances), you will need to employ a plumber or heating engineer. See the section *Employing contractors* in Chapter 3 above.

Before deciding on the type of heating you want, you will need to consider the following:

- When the heat is needed. For example, if the property is empty during the day, storage heaters would be a poor choice as they would be at their most effective when nobody is there to enjoy them.
- If the system needs to heat water as well, how much hot water do you use? A small household might decide in favour of a combination boiler which heats water as it is needed, instead of a system that

stores hot water in a cylinder, although the latter has the advantages of an airing cupboard and an immersion heater in the event of boiler breakdown.

- The cost of installation. It may be cheaper to upgrade what you already have than to replace it completely.
- The running costs. Portable electric fires are expensive to run continuously compared with other forms of heating, but could be cost effective for a little extra warmth in one or two rooms occasionally.
- The fuel needed. You may not have mains gas, or facilities for storing coal or oil, limiting the options available.
- The type of building (house, bungalow, flat) and the system best suited to each.
- The amount of disruption. You may need to redecorate, or at least touch up, if removing the boiler or replacing old radiators with smaller new ones.

Different types of heating have advantages and disadvantages over others, but the bottom line will usually be the cost of installation and the running costs.

Remember that even central-heating systems fuelled by gas or oil have electrically powered controls so that in a power cut you may lose heating as well as lighting and perhaps cooking and hot water.

• Mains gas
A clean and popular fuel for central heating, mains gas is available to most households except in some rural locations. Unlike LPG (see below), mains gas is 'on tap' constantly from the supplier, and, unlike electricity, there is little chance of disruption to supply. One of the cheapest forms of heating to install and run.

• Oil
Oil is usually used in homes where mains gas is not available. The oil is delivered into a storage tank in the garden or outbuilding. The oil is then used to fire a boiler which heats radiators and usually water as well. The

storage tank can be plastic or steel. If it is to be installed more than 30-40 metres from the road, you should consult your local fuel suppliers to make sure they can get access for delivery. Oil-fired boilers are clean and efficient and less expensive to run than other fuels in most areas, although installation costs are usually more expensive than for mains gas. Shop around for competitive fuel prices.

• LPG

LPG (Liquefied Petroleum Gas) is another alternative for homes which are not connected to mains gas. The gas is delivered into a tank in much the same way as oil, and then fires a boiler which heats radiators and hot water. Strict rules apply as to where the pressurized storage tank can be situated and it must usually be visible from the road, so not all homes have a suitable place to site one. Local fuel suppliers, who also supply and lease storage tanks, should be consulted for current regulations. The fuel is clean and efficient, but running costs are much more expensive than oil.

• Solid fuel

Solid-fuel boilers perform the same function as any others, but have lots of disadvantages. The temperature drops when cleaning or adding fuel, there is a lot of dust and dirt, and the boiler has to be manually refuelled at regular intervals. The coal is delivered to order into suitable storage facilities, but the user must physically bring it into the home by the bucket-load for use. If wood is used, this can also be delivered, but wood does not give off as much heat as coal. Heating appliances could be a back boiler or room heater with back boiler. Aga and Rayburn are popular makes of solid fuel appliance, although nowadays they are more often run on oil, gas or electricity than on solid fuel. They are expensive to buy and install, but will probably outlive the owner. The best combination is probably an Aga or Rayburn cooker and water heater and a separate boiler for central heating and water heating in summer.

• Electric storage heaters

A form of heating using electricity, storage heaters contain insulating blocks which are heated overnight. The blocks then gradually release this heat during the day, which means that by the time evening comes most of the heat has gone (unless you live in Scotland, where a booster period during the day tops up the temperature). Although you can alter the amount of heat taken into the blocks and the rate at which it is released, the units do not respond efficiently to room temperature fluctuations. The heaters use electricity during off-peak hours at a cheaper rate per unit, but this is still a comparatively expensive form of heating to run. The advantage of storage heaters is that installation is quick, comparatively cheap and less disruptive than most other forms of heating.

• Portable heaters
Portable heaters are a good source of instant heat, but the appliance needs to be run continually to keep the temperature constant, especially if the room is poorly insulated. Electric bar heaters and fan heaters are relatively cheap to buy but expensive to run. Installation is cheap and instant – fit a plug and away you go – so the kind of disruption experienced when pipes and electric cables are laid is avoided. Second-hand portable heaters, especially those fuelled by bottled gas, can often be found for sale in local newspapers. It is obviously very important to make sure these appliances are in good working order before using.

Whatever form of heating you choose, the air supply should comply strictly with the regulations and requirements of the appliance. Air supply vents should not be covered at any time.

Kitchen improvement or replacement
Undoubtedly one of the most important rooms in a home, the kitchen is often top of the list for improvement or replacement, and the number of retailers selling kitchen units shows how popular they are and how often they are replaced.

A replacement kitchen is an expensive addition, so if you are contemplating this, you want to make sure you get the most for your money. Not only are there the services offered by carpenters and specialist kitchen builders, but many general furniture stores and even

DIY stores now sell kitchens of all types. At any time, at least one major furniture retailer can be found advertising 'huge discounts' on fitted kitchens, but don't worry if you miss the closing date for one of these unmissable offers – there is usually another in a week or two. Many stores offer a free kitchen-planning service, giving you the benefit of computer planning to experiment with different layouts to make best use of available space. You will usually be given a printout of the final plan and a quotation of costs, which you can then use to judge estimates from other retailers for the same goods and services to make sure the price is competitive.

The cheapest fitted units are invariably 'flat packed' for self-assembly. This can seem a relatively simple task when you first glance at the instructions. You just need to screw panel A to the left side of panel B, then glue the front of drawer E onto the wooden dowels of each side J and K. A piece of cake, you might think, but these things are never quite as simple as they look, and panel B might not fit exactly onto panel A, and gluing the dowels is a bit of a problem in the absence of said glue. However, flat-packed furniture and kitchen units have improved greatly over the years, and whilst they still take time and patience to assemble, they look as good and are just as sturdy as the ready-assembled alternatives which cost much more.

DID YOU KNOW?   *Most fitted kitchen units have a similar carcass – only the doors are different.*

The price of a new kitchen rarely includes fitting, which can account for around a third again of the cost of the kitchen itself. Even if the units come fully assembled, they still need to be fixed to the walls (a deceptively difficult DIY job for the inexperienced), and unless the new units are a straight 'out and in' replacement, there is likely to be some plumbing and electrical work involved. The cost of employ-ing a plumber and/or electrician needs to be added to the cost of the kitchen units to get a fair estimation of the total amount, and don't forget the extras like a new sink, taps, lighting, tiling and flooring which add even more. Most kitchen retailers employ or subcontract a fitter, but you are not normally obliged to employ the retailer's fitter, so other quotes should be obtained to be sure of a fair deal.

Unless the existing kitchen is beyond redemption, upgrading it might be a much cheaper option than total replacement. You can make a remarkable difference by simply replacing the sink and installing new worktops, or by painting the doors of the units. You need to use suitable paint for this and prepare the surfaces well, but if the job is done properly and the paint is washable it should last for many years. If the units themselves are not the problem, the decoration could be updated with a coat of paint or new tiles.

Because fitted units are so expensive, it is often cheaper to buy items of free-standing furniture, and this way you can add to the arrangement as you can afford it, rather than buying everything in one go. You can also take the furniture with you if you ever sell the property, which you cannot normally do with a fitted kitchen.

Bathroom improvement or replacement

The cost of bathroom suites varies enormously, and whilst you can spend a small fortune at the luxury end of the market, it is perfectly possible to buy a new suite for a few hundred pounds. The impact of a suite on the appearance of the bathroom, because of the sheer size of the items, means that replacing a dilapidated suite gives an immediate transformation. Replacing a suite involves some plumbing, but if the positioning of the new items is the same as for the existing ones, this is kept to a minimum. Adding extra items like a shower or bidet involves more plumbing, so it is always advisable to obtain quotes for the plumbing work involved before you buy any items, as this can be more expensive than the items themselves.

If the existing suite is in reasonable condition and funds are limited, it might be better to improve the look of the room with fresh paint (see below) and new towels, shower curtain, window blind, etc. rather than replacing the suite.

If the decoration has seen better days, you will probably want to redecorate. This is not a problem if the existing decoration is wallpaper or paint, and redecorating a comparatively small area like a bathroom is a fairly quick project. However, if the walls are tiled and you want to remove or replace them, this can present something of a challenge. The prospect of removing tiles is not a happy one, and the amount of work involved in turning a previously tiled wall into a suitable surface for paint or paper is enormous, especially since the condition of the wall underneath the tiles may be less than perfect. If this turns out to be the case, you may find yourself wishing you had never started. If you decide to try your hand at re-tiling, you will find that it is not as easy as it looks. Having successfully tiled a floor, I found my own confidence was boosted into tackling a bathroom wall. I soon discovered, though, the difference between tiling a floor and a wall – tiles on the floor stay where you lay them!

A far easier and quicker alternative is simply to paint the original tiles. They need to be thoroughly cleaned and prepared before the paint is applied, and certain products work better than others. A good decorating supplier will be able to advise which paints are most suitable to ensure a good final result.

DID YOU KNOW?   *One of the best surfaces for tiling is tiles.*

Showers are increasingly popular, and since they use less water than a bath, and so less fuel, the cost of installing one can pay for itself over time. However, although the shower unit itself may be quite inexpensive, installation involves electrical work as well as plumbing if the shower is electrically operated (which most of the good ones are), so the installation costs are likely to far exceed the purchase cost. A cheaper alternative is the type of shower fitment which uses water direct from the taps, but these are not as effective at maintaining an even water-temperature, and many people have been unexpectedly doused with freezing water when a tap is used somewhere else in the system. A very unpleasant way to start the day.

If you have the space, an en suite bathroom or shower room is a pleasant addition to any home, and is especially welcome if your household has outgrown the family bathroom. However, the relatively small cost of the fitments can lead one to imagine that the project will be less expensive than it actually turns out to be. The fitments account for only a small percentage of the actual cost. On top of this you need to allow for plumbing and electrical work as well as the obvious cost of separating an area into the en suite room. Add to that new floor covering, decorating and items like lighting, and the project quickly becomes a major expense. Another factor which can cause problems and additional expense is the provision of adequate ventilation, which is a requirement of building regulations.

> **DID YOU KNOW?** *Building approval or consent may be required when installing or altering the position of a WC, bath etc., or where there is new drainage or plumbing.*

Consents

Before making alterations or improvements to your home, you should first ascertain whether you need permission from your local authority, and/or whether the work will need to be inspected to see that it meets building standards. The following information will give you some idea of what is involved, but it would be impossible to detail in full the working practices of all authorities up and down the country since some have different procedures and requirements. If you are considering any building work whatsoever, check with your local authority to find out if permission or approval is required, and if so, what specific steps are needed to obtain it.

Many people confuse planning permission with building regulations approval (known in Scotland as building control approval), assuming they are the same thing. In fact they cover two distinct areas of legislation, and although some building projects may need both planning permission and building regulations approval, obtaining one does not automatically guarantee the other. When both are required, and given that planning permission may demand changes in design, it is sometimes better to obtain permission before preparing the detailed information needed to obtain approval.

Planning permission

The local authority planning department is generally concerned with the appearance of properties and their use, and controls can be decided by local policy as much as by detailed regulation, so different areas may have different rules. Local authorities tread a difficult path in their efforts to protect the character of their area whilst still giving individual homeowners reasonable freedom to alter their property. As a general rule, any addition or change which alters or affects the external appearance of a property may need planning permission. In some parts of the country this includes minor additions like satellite television aerials.

If permission is not granted, you may need to carry out retrospective remedial work or even face the prospect of enforced demolition.

DID YOU KNOW?   *Some councils issue design guides to assist in the designing of a building or extension.*

When considering a building project, you first need to find out if a planning application is actually necessary, by contacting the planning department of your local council. It is essential that you do this before starting any work. As general guidance only, planning permission is usually necessary in any of the following instances:

- The property is to be divided into separate dwellings.
- The property is to be divided to provide commercial or business accommodation.
- A caravan is to be placed in the grounds for use as a dwelling.
- You want to erect something which is contrary to the building's original planning permission.

- The work could obstruct the view of road users or requires the provision of, or extension of, access to a major road.

If the work does not fall into any of the above, but your home is a listed building or is situated in a conservation area (or an area of outstanding natural beauty), or if conditions have been imposed on it to restrict changes, you may still need to apply for planning permission.

Applying for planning permission

> ### TAKE A TIP
> If, having made verbal enquiries to the council, you are told that the proposal will not require planning permission, it is still advisable to get written confirmation from the planning department to safeguard against a future dispute.

If the alteration requires planning permission, you will need to complete the necessary application form(s) and submit the required fee in order for the proposal to be processed. Before completing forms and writing out cheques for fees, it might be useful to discuss the proposal in detail with the local authority to see if the application is likely to be refused. You can then decide whether making the application would be worthwhile.

You may decide to make an outline application first to obtain permission in principle before going to the trouble of preparing detailed drawings or plans, although these will be required later for a full application. The council will advise what drawings are needed.

The planning department will usually acknowledge receipt of an application within a few days, and will then place it on the Planning Register so that it is open to inspection by members of the public. The department may also contact your neighbours or put up a site notice to ascertain local opinion and may advertise the proposals in the local press. In Scotland you are required to inform your neighbours of an application.

If your building proposal raises written objections, you can usually have sight of these at the council offices or ask for copies.

Building regulations

In order to ensure that the design, construction and use of a building is safe, is not a fire hazard, is damp-proof and rain-proof, and has adequate ventilation, access, heat insulation and toilet facilities, building control officers inspect certain building work to check that it conforms to complex rules designed to ensure public and personal safety. Alterations must comply with minimum building specifications, the building materials used must be suitable, and the building method must be satisfactory. Not every structural alteration needs building regulation approval, but if, after the work has been carried out, it transpires that it was needed, perfectly satisfactory work may need to be undone simply to prove that it was carried out according to regulations in the first place.

You will be able to ascertain from the local authority whether the planned alterations need approval. It is imperative that local authority guidance is sought for individual cases, but below is a broad guide to those alterations or additions which usually require approval and those which do not.

Approval is generally required for the following:

- all building work
- loft conversions
- garage conversions to living accommodation
- internal alterations such as removing a wall to turn two rooms into one
- conversion from single dwelling into flats
- cavity wall insulation
- installation of gas, solid fuel or oil heating appliances
- installation of fittings which require new plumbing, e.g. a WC.

Approval is generally NOT required for the following:

- replacement windows
- car port
- conservatory

- porch
- minor repairs
- erection of a boundary wall
- installation of fittings, unless requiring new drainage or plumbing.

Having ascertained that building regulation approval is required, you will need to supply the local authority with information about the planned work, usually in the form of either a full plan or building notice. Check with your local planning department for the necessary procedure.

DID YOU KNOW? *If you are planning to erect scaffolding or place a skip on the public highway (this includes pavements and grass verges as well as roads), you may need a licence from the highway authority (roads authority in Scotland).*

You can probably submit your own plan so long as it conforms to certain requirements, mainly that it is to a recognized scale, includes construction notes and all major dimensions, and that proposed work is clearly distinguishable from the original building. Alternatively you could enlist the services of an architect or surveyor. Once the plan has been checked and approved, the authority will issue an Approval Notice. On completion of the work to the requirements of the regulations, a completion certificate can (and should) be obtained (see below).

Building notices can be submitted instead of a full plan, but these are not acceptable for all types of application. A site plan will probably be required and further details may be requested at a later date. It is worth checking with the authority that they will issue a completion certificate under this procedure. A building notice generally saves time, because there are no plans which require approval by the local authority. However because of this an approval notice will not be given, so you or your builder need to work closely with the building control officer to avoid potential problems. With both a full plan and building notices, a fee is payable to the authority, the amount of which depends on the type of work.

Completion Certificate

It is important to indicate when obtaining building regulations approval that a completion certificate is required. This certificate is your proof that the building work has been carried out correctly in accordance with the requirements of Building Standards, and is an important document if the property is ever sold. Without this document, the standard of the work may be questioned and anyone considering buying the property will have doubts that the building is sound. The authority will only issue the certificate when it is in receipt of all statutory notifications.

> **DID YOU KNOW?** *A proposed change of access from a public road, e.g. a new driveway, may require approval by the highways department (in England and Wales) or the roads authority (in Scotland).*

The title deeds of a house or flat frequently contain strict conditions about the structure of the building and may rule out the possibility of certain additions or alterations. With a leasehold flat, for example, the landlord may refuse permission for the addition of a dividing wall. Although it is sometimes possible (at a cost) to get agreement or authority to change these restrictions, you should make sure that you are permitted to implement the intended alterations before proceeding with the work.

It is worth reiterating that if you ever want to sell your property, you can encounter lengthy delays and major headaches if you do not have the relevant documents to show that an improvement or addition has any necessary planning permission, building regulations approval, completion certificate and authority of the title.

Grants

Some improvements and repairs are eligible for grant aid through the local council. The types of grant available vary according to area and are usually subject to some form of means testing. A renovation grant is mainly for raising the standard of the property, by for example installing a bathroom where previously there was none. This type of grant is usually only available for properties built or converted over 10 years ago.

If you obtain a grant and subsequently sell the property, you may have to repay some or all of the funds received. For example, if there are stipulations that the grant must be repaid proportionately if the property is sold within three years, you will have to repay two thirds if you sell within a year, one third if you sell within two years, but nothing if you sell after three years. Be sure to retain any documents relating to grants since you may need to present them if the property is sold.

5. FINANCING SPENDING

Having looked in the last chapter at improving your home, you may be asking yourself how you could fund such improvements, and you might be considering some sort of loan, so below is a brief summary of some of the finance options available. A subject of such complexity cannot be dealt with fully here, so it is important to stress that you must be aware of your obligations as a borrower. Always read the small print before you sign anything, and make sure you understand it.

Loans

Nowadays loans can be arranged quickly and easily (some would say too easily), often over the telephone, and finance companies advertise their services widely. The money can be used for almost anything, so even if the loan is secured on your home, you do not necessarily have to plough the money back into the property.

A *secured loan* is held against a specific asset owned by you. If you default on the loan, the creditor can lay claim to this asset. In the case of an *unsecured loan*, the creditor cannot claim against a specific asset, although he can still sue for default. A mortgage, for example, is a secured loan with the property being held as security. If you fail to keep up your repayments, the lender can lay claim on the property and sell it to recover the debt. A secured loan carries the standard warning 'Your home is at risk if you do not keep up repayments on a mortgage or other loan secured on it'.

> **DID YOU KNOW?** *Secured loans are usually cheaper than unsecured loans.*

When applying for a loan, you will be asked dozens of questions about your income, employment, personal details, mortgage details, existing credit arrangements, and many more, either over the telephone or on an application form. The finance company or bank then considers this information to determine whether you are creditworthy, by using a credit scoring method. To apply for a loan you usually have to be aged 18 or over. If your credit score meets the minimum required, the loan is granted. The finance company or bank may also use the services of a credit reference agency to check that you do not have a history of bad debt. It is still possible to obtain a loan with a history of debt (a 'history' could be non-payment of community charge or other bill), by approaching finance companies who deal specifically with 'high risk' borrowers, but these companies usually charge a higher rate of interest than other lenders, and require security.

You do not have to be an existing customer of a particular bank to apply to it for a loan (although most people are), but you will usually be asked to open a current account to service the loan if the application is accepted.

If you shop around for a loan, look for the APR (Annual Percentage Rate) to compare costs. This figure gives a clear picture of what you actually have to pay, including any fees and charges. The APR usually decreases the more you borrow. If the rate is fixed, the amount payable each month remains the same. The length of time over which you elect to repay the loan affects the total amount repayable – the longer you borrow the money for, the more interest is paid over the term of the loan, although the monthly repayments are lower. If you repay a loan early, you may have to pay a charge of around one month's interest.

Flexible loans are useful if you do not want to use all the borrowed money straight away, but they are generally more expensive than borrowing a lump sum over a fixed term.

Overdrafts

An overdraft is another method of borrowing, although you may have to clear the overdraft within six months. An overdraft should be arranged with the bank in advance (an agreed overdraft), rather than withdrawing money on an empty account, otherwise an additional charge may be made. Overdrafts have an EPR (Effective Annual Rate) which does not include bank charges or monthly fees payable on top of interest.

> **DID YOU KNOW?** *Tax relief does not apply to overdraft or credit card borrowing.*

Remortgaging and secured loans

If you have sufficient equity in your property, i.e. the market value of the property is in excess of any existing loan (or mortgage) secured on it, you may prefer to release the equity by increasing your mortgage. Alternatively you can keep your mortgage the same, but secure a separate loan on the property. These arrangements usually involve a valuation of the property by the lender, which you will have to pay for, and you could also face some legal and arrangement fees.

Buying on credit

Credit cards

Credit cards are a convenient way to 'borrow' because you do not need to make special arrangements every time you make a purchase. Each month you receive a statement showing the amount owing and the date by which a minimum payment is due. Interest rates are comparatively high (look at the APR), but if you use a credit card as a method of short term borrowing and pay off the entire debt each month, you avoid paying interest. You do, however, usually have to pay an annual fee.

Credit card purchases over £100 give consumers added protection against shoddy goods, because a claim can be made against the card company as well as, or instead of, the supplier, which is particularly useful if the supplier is no longer trading. Retailers who accept payment by credit cards pay a service charge to the credit card company, so some offer a discount for customers using cash.

When using a credit card, always check the sales voucher details before signing; in particular make sure the amount payable has been entered and is correct. If you lose your card or it is stolen, advise the card company immediately. Until you do so, you will be liable if someone else uses it without your permission. Liability in such cases is limited to £50, but if you knowingly allow someone else to use your card, you will be liable for whatever bills they run up.

Debit cards like Switch, and cash cards, do not give credit. The amount of the purchase or withdrawal of cash is deducted from your account in much the same way as when using a cheque, only more quickly.

TAKE A TIP
Retailers often give credit, but if you borrow from your bank for the purchase and go back to the retailer with cash, you might be able to negotiate a better deal on the price.

Hire purchase and credit sales

With an HP arrangement, you effectively hire the goods and pay for them in instalments. You have use of the goods whilst they are being paid for, but cannot sell them until all the instalments have been paid. Some retailers finance HP arrangements themselves, but a common arrangement is for the retailer to sell the goods to a finance company which then hires them to you under the HP agreement.

If you fall behind with your payments, the finance company can repossess the goods, but must apply to the courts for repossession if you have paid a third or more of the credit price.

The main difference between credit sales and HP is that goods sold on credit belong to you when you take possession of them, although you have not paid for them in full. You can sell the goods before you have finished paying for them, although if you do this you may have to settle the outstanding debt in one go. If you fall behind with payments, the goods cannot be repossessed, but the finance company can sue you for the amount owing.

As well as repaying the cost of the goods, if you use HP or credit arrangements you will be charged interest. The amount of interest varies, and in practice the retailer or finance company can charge whatever rate they like. They should make sure you are fully aware of the interest rate, and it must be clearly displayed in advertisements and on any agreement.

The APR (Annual Percentage Rate) is the one to look out for and use as a comparison, because it gives a more realistic account of what you will actually pay, including charges in addition to the interest rate itself. If the APR is not fixed, the agreement should say so.

6. INSURANCE

Simply put, insurance is a way of providing financial protection (*cover*) against possible loss or damage. It is not a safeguard against a certainty, but rather against a possibility.

As a homeowner, you will generally have two types of insurance – one to cover the property itself (buildings insurance), and the other to cover your possessions inside it (contents insurance). Whilst buildings insurance is compulsory if you have a mortgage or other loan secured on the building, the decision whether or not to take out contents insurance is up to the individual. Some people choose not to.

Insurance is paid for by payments of a *premium*, often in monthly instalments. The amount of the premium will depend on the value of the insured item(s). Once agreement is made to pay the premium, the terms of the policy are accepted. Read through the proposal form carefully and make sure you have disclosed all relevant information. Withholding such information, even if it is not specifically requested by the insurers, could invalidate the policy in the event of a claim. When you renew a policy you are implying that the policy details are unchanged.

Your insurance company will issue you with a policy document, which sets out the terms and conditions of the insurance. This policy shows the sum insured (the total amount the company will pay out if goods or building are totally destroyed), and the amount of the premium payments.

Contents insurance

What is covered?

Contents insurance covers your possessions whilst they are in your home. Most policies do not cover possessions when they are off the premises, as might be the case with the contents of a briefcase or handbag. Additional cover is needed for this, which can be arranged as an extension to the original policy and is usually referred to as an 'all risks' policy.

Insurance policies generally cover against loss or damage outside the

198

control of the owner, but if you wish to insure against accidental damage, extra cover might be needed. Most standard policies cover for such eventualities as:

- Fire
- Flood/storm damage
- Theft
- Explosion
- Earthquake
- Subsidence/landslide
- Heating-oil leaks
- Water damage
- Malicious damage/riot
- Impact from falling trees, aircraft, vehicles

Some policies cover more than this, some less, so it is important to read the policy document carefully and make sure you understand it fully. All policies have exclusions, and whilst insurance would probably be the last thing on your mind in the event of some of them (nuclear contamination and war for example), it is important that you are aware of anything which could invalidate the cover you believe you have.

High-value items like jewellery, antiques or certain musical instruments need to be insured separately if their value exceeds the policy limit, and an independent valuation may be required in such cases.

DID YOU KNOW? *If you cancel an insurance agreement, you may still have to pay the full premium.*

Policies are either *new-for-old* or *indemnity*. Under a new-for-old policy, the insurance company pays a sufficient amount to replace lost or damaged goods with new ones. Under an indemnity policy, the insurance company will only pay the value of goods after taking into account the age and condition.

> **DID YOU KNOW?** *Clothing and household linen is never insured on a new-for-old basis.*

An *excess* is the first part of the claim which the customer agrees to forego. If the excess amount is £50, the insurance company will only pay out on claims in excess of £50 and does not pay the first £50 of any claim. If you accept a high excess, the insurance company may offer you discounted premium payments.

> **DID YOU KNOW?** *Some insurance companies offer a reduction of the premium if you take action to secure your home against burglary.*

How much should you insure for?

To calculate the figure your contents need to be insured for, make a list of all your possessions, including those in the garden shed, garage and loft, and the amount each item would cost to replace at today's prices. Then add all these figures together. If your policy is index-linked it will take account of inflation, but if it is not you should add a percentage amount to cover inflation for the year ahead. You will also need to review the sum insured each year. If you add significantly to your possessions after taking out the policy, you should advise the insurance company so that it can increase the sum insured.

> **DID YOU KNOW?** *When renewing your existing insurance arrangements, you have a duty to disclose any relevant changes which might affect the policy. If you do not, the insurance could be invalidated.*

Making a claim

If you need to make a claim, contact your insurance company, which will send you a claim form for completion. The insurance company may then instruct one of its representatives to visit and report back with details of the loss. If, for example, you have a new-for-old policy and are claiming a new 3-piece suite because paint was accidentally spilt over one of the chairs, the claims adjuster will inspect the suite to determine whether it could be cleaned or repaired, or if the whole suite would have to be replaced.

You may need to prove the loss. If the claim is a result of burglary or other theft, the insurance company will ask for confirmation that the police have been informed, and you must do this regardless of whether you think your goods will be recovered. The police will issue you with a crime reference number to quote on the claim form.

Buildings insurance

You need to take out adequate buildings insurance to safeguard against possible loss if the building is destroyed or damaged. Once contracts have been exchanged for the purchase of the property (in Scotland, once missives have been concluded), you are responsible for the insurance of the building. This will be a requirement of your mortgage, although an exception to this would be if the property being purchased was under construction at the time of exchange, in which case your solicitor should check that the builder had insured the unfinished building. Lenders usually arrange buildings insurance of the properties they lend against. You can alternatively make your own arrangements, but the lenders will want to check the policy, and will probably charge you a fee for this.

If the property is leasehold, the freeholder will usually insure the building and charge each leaseholder a proportion of the premium to reimburse the cost. Flat-owners need insurance to cover not only their individual living premises but also any other parts of the block they have a liability to maintain.

If you buy a freehold without a mortgage or any other loan secured on the property, you are not obliged to insure it (unlike car insurance, property insurance is not a legal requirement), but the risks of not insuring will be unacceptable to most people.

INSURANCE

What is covered?

Policies differ between insurance companies, so you need to check exactly what your policy covers, but most insure against the following:

- fire
- flood
- lightning/storm damage
- theft
- explosion
- earthquake
- subsidence/landslide
- heating-oil leaks
- water damage
- malicious damage/riot
- impact from falling trees, aircraft, vehicles

It is important to check the policy to see what exclusions apply. There are bound to be some which may surprise. For example, greenhouses are usually covered, but fences are not. As well as the actual building, some of the internal fixtures like bathroom suites and fitted furniture, e.g. kitchen units, are likely to be covered by the buildings insurance.

As with contents insurance, you are usually required to pay the first part of a claim (the excess), although this may not apply to all claims. If you want extra cover for something which does not appear in the policy, like temporary accommodation if damage to your home makes it uninhabitable, speak to your insurers to see if they can extend the cover to include this.

How much should you insure for?

The sum insured (the maximum amount the insurance company will pay if the worst comes to the worst) needs to be accurate. If your house was surveyed before you bought it, the surveyor's report will probably give a buildings insurance figure. However, it is up to you to make sure the amount is sufficient; remember that the figure must cover the cost of *rebuilding*, not of buying a comparable property, and this could be more costly. Your insurance company will probably have up-to-date tables to help you make an accurate calculation.

If the policy is index-linked, the sum insured is automatically adjusted to take account of inflation or other matters which could affect rebuilding costs. If the policy is not index-linked, you need to recalculate periodically. If you make significant improvements or alterations to your home, you must advise the insurance company so that it can make any necessary adjustments to your policy.

Making a claim

In theory, the first thing to do in the event of damage is to contact your insurance company before making or arranging for any repairs. The exception to this might be if a storm brings your chimney down in the middle of the night, in which case you might need to make repairs as a matter of urgency. Some insurance companies have 24-hour help-lines to offer advice and assistance in such circumstances, but if your insurers are not contactable at the time of damage, most of them will agree to reimburse you the costs of temporary repairs, especially if the action you took prevented further damage.

In the event of a claim, the insurance company sends a claim form for completion and then arranges for one of its representatives to visit the property to assess the damage and make sure the claim is reasonable. You will be asked to obtain quotes for the work, and these need to be approved by the insurers before work commences. Naturally the insurers will favour the lowest quote, and this is the payment they will make to you, less any excess.

Disputes

Insurance companies may refuse to pay out in the event of a claim, if they consider you have withheld relevant facts or have not complied with the terms of the policy. The Insurance Ombudsman Bureau (Tel: 0171 928 7600) may be able to settle a dispute between insurer and customer, but they usually only become involved as a last resort when communication between the two parties has reached a stalemate. If after investigating the case the ombudsman rules in your favour, the insurer must abide by the ruling. You, however, can take the matter further if the ruling goes against you.

Sometimes an insurance company offers to make an ex-gratia payment, which is its way of settling a claim (with a lesser payment than that claimed for), as an act of goodwill.

7. SECURITY

Security at the door

Although over 90% of thefts from homes occur when the building is unoccupied, most of the others occur because the perpetrators are invited in. Con-men think up some ingenious tricks, so a healthy suspicion of any uninvited caller is needed.

Firstly, see whom you are opening the door to by looking out of the window or through a spy hole if you have one. If it is dark, turn on an outside light to illuminate the doorstep and the caller. Always use a door chain before opening the door. If you do not already have a door chain, consider having one fitted. If the caller is not known to you, be very wary of inviting him into your home. This includes 'emergency' requests to use your telephone (you can offer to make the call yourself), and don't be fooled into a false sense of security if the caller is a woman or child, or claims to represent a religious or charitable organization.

> **DID YOU KNOW?** *Some service organizations operate a password system to protect their customers. When a representative of the company calls, you can check that he or she is genuine by asking for the pre-arranged password as identification.*

Salesmen who 'cold call' without appointment are best turned away. Don't enter into a discussion on the doorstep about whatever they are selling, and don't consider allowing them in. Instead, thank them politely for calling then close the door. If they are selling something which you are interested in, look up the telephone number of the company in the phone book after the salesman has gone and arrange a proper appointment. If the salesman gives you a business card, check in the 'phone directory that such a business exists before telephoning to arrange an appointment. If the caller is not genuine, the number on the card could be an accomplice.

Genuine representatives of service organizations who might have good reason to call (the gas man or telephone engineer for example) have identity cards. However, if you do not know what the legitimate card looks like (and who does?) how do you know if it is a fake? A tatty piece of card with just a name printed on it could be suspect – most identity cards are plastic-coated with a recognisable logo and often the caller's photograph. Do not be fooled if the caller claims to have lost his card or left it at home.

If you have any doubt, ask the caller to wait outside, close the door, then look up the telephone number of the company or organization he or she is claiming to represent and check that there is a record of the visit. A genuine caller will not mind waiting on the doorstep while you do this, so don't be rushed into letting someone in without checking because he or she claims to be in a hurry. Even if your telephone call confirms the caller is who he says he is, it is still not a good idea to leave any stranger alone whilst in your home.

A professional conman 'works' a street, calling at each house in turn until he strikes lucky. Tell your neighbours if you have an uninvited caller who acts suspiciously, so that they are forewarned when he comes knocking on their door, and telephone the police.

As well as unscrupulous callers looking to steal your possessions, there are those who call uninvited offering to carry out work. They may be looking to gain entry to your home to steal from you, or they may take money from you in advance of doing a job, never to be seen again. To avoid this happening to you, don't employ casual callers without first checking their credentials, and it is not advisable to sign anything on the doorstep.

Don't open the door without using the DOORSTEP code:
Observe first – look through a window or door-viewer.
Only open your door after connecting a chain or limiter.
Refuse entry if you are not satisfied.
Switch on an outside light when it's dark to see who's there.
Think 'thief' – don't leave strangers alone in your home.
Examine identity cards – genuine officials always have them.
Protect yourself – if unsure contact the police or neighbour.

Beating burglary

The bad news is that a professional burglar can get past almost any window lock, door bolt or domestic security system, no matter how comprehensive or expensive. The good news is that the vast majority of burglars are not professionals. They are opportunists who choose soft targets, and this type of attack is often preventable with some commonsense precautions.

Windows and doors

Even if you do not have window locks or the added security of deadlocks on doors, the first rule to guard against the burglar is to make sure doors and windows are closed. This may sound obvious, but since around 20% of burglaries occur because the homeowner left open a door or window, it is a point worthy of mention.

Five-lever mortice deadlocks are the type of door locks recommended by the police, but if you go to the trouble of fitting one, be sure you use it. This type of lock can only be opened with a key, so even if a burglar gets into your home through a window, he cannot carry your possessions out through the door. This is also true of an automatic deadlock, which works like a normal latch in that the door locks as it is pulled closed, but it can also be double-locked with a key, making it impossible to open from inside. If you use a deadlock from inside, make sure you can easily get to the key in an emergency.

You might also consider bolts at the top and bottom of doors, but make sure these are positioned so that they cannot be reached through a part-glazed door if the glass is broken, and use strong screws. Glazed doors are vulnerable, so you might consider replacing ordinary glass with laminated glass, which is much stronger. UPVC doors and windows and glazed patio doors are more difficult to secure, so get professional advice from a reputable locksmith.

Window locks are particularly important on downstairs windows and those which are easily accessed from the ground, e.g. are next to a fire escape easily reached from a flat roof. Windows which are hidden from view give a burglar shelter and plenty of time to enter without being noticed by neighbours or passers-by, so these should also have special attention. A good window lock means the burglar has to break the glass to get in. He will not want to do this because the noise could draw attention to him.

Window locks can be bought from most DIY stores for little cost, and fitting them is usually a simple job. They can be embedded into a wooden frame so that they are hidden, but it is worth remembering that visible locks may deter a burglar. If he can get into somewhere else more easily, he will probably give your property a miss.

Don't make the common mistake of leaving the key to a window lock on the window sill, so that a burglar may break the glass then reach the key to unlock the window. You should, however, make sure you and your family know where the keys are, and they should be easily accessed in case you need to get out in an emergency.

Keys

Whilst it is useful to leave a spare front-door key with a neighbour in case you lock yourself out, make sure it is stored safely, in particular that it is not labelled with your name or address. Never hide a spare key under the doormat or flower pot, or hang one from a string behind the letterbox. Burglars know from experience all the usual, and unusual, places people use to hide keys.

When moving into a new home, you might like to consider changing the existing door lock or having an additional one fitted, because you have no idea who the previous owners gave spare keys to, or if they relinquished all of them to you.

> **DID YOU KNOW?**   *Most burglaries occur during the afternoon and early evening.*

Valuables

If your possessions were stolen, could you give an accurate description of them? Most people couldn't. Think about it – do you know the make and model of your computer or TV? Could you identify your jewellery so that there could be no doubt that it was yours? Probably not. So, if the police discovered your possessions, how would they know they were yours? Because of these problems, it makes sense to mark and/or photograph your possessions and keep a note of serial numbers.

There are several different methods of marking. If you want your possessions marked so that the mark itself is a deterrent to burglars (marked goods are difficult to dispose of), you will want the identification to be obvious and of a type which would depreciate the value of the item if removed. This type of marking – punching or engraving – might be used on garden and electrical equipment. If this method would damage the item or reduce its value, using an ultra-violet pen to mark the base might be a better alternative. This type of mark is invisible until a UV lamp is shone on it, so the appearance of, say, a clock or ornament is not marred. The mark left by a UV pen fades with time and can be washed off, so for china and glass a better alternative would be a ceramic marking pen which does not scratch the surface but is permanent.

The best identification mark to use on your possessions is your postcode. Quite simply, a postcode is smaller than an address but still gives the police, on recovering property, details of the rightful owner. Since the postcode does not identify an individual property, but rather only a section of a road or village, you should also add the first letters of your house name or number. So, if your address is 11 Rocket Square, London EC2V 2QP, your identification mark would be EC2V 2QP 11.

TAKE A TIP

Display a 'Coded for keeps' sticker (available from local police stations) prominently on a window or door of your home, to make your possessions unattractive to burglars.

Photographing your possessions, especially those too delicate, valuable or difficult to mark (antiques and jewellery for example), enables you to identify them properly if they are recovered by the police.

A photograph should be taken of each item individually (not a snapshot of the room including the item) and it may be necessary to take more than one in order to show anything which distinguishes the item in more detail, such as a scratch on the underside of a table. It also helps to include a ruler in the shot to indicate size.

The record of your possessions, including undeveloped photographs (the film only needs to be developed if the items are stolen), should be kept in a safe place.

> **DID YOU KNOW?** *Your local police station has plenty of free leaflets on all aspects of crime prevention.*

Prevention

No one wants their home to be a fortress against the outside world, so whilst additional locks and security systems are a hindrance to the thief it is better to stop your home being a target in the first place by taking preventative action.

An occupied property is far less likely to be a target for burglary than an unoccupied one, so try to make it look as though there is always someone at home; a time switch which turns on lights as dusk falls is a good idea if you are often late coming home from work. You can even get a gadget which automatically opens and closes the curtains. If you leave lights on when going out, choose those which you usually have on when at home, like the bedroom and/or lounge, and not just the hall or an outside light. You could also leave a radio on, tuned in to a non-music channel like Radio 4. Whenever you go out, makes sure all the access doors are locked and the windows are closed and preferably also locked. Internal doors are best left unlocked to avoid unnecessary damage if the property is burgled.

As well as making your home look unattractive to burglars, you can also make entry difficult by employing some home defence. Firstly you will need to identify your home's weak spots. Put yourself in the thief's shoes and imagine you have no front door key. Walk around the outside of your home and see if you can get back in. Have you left the bathroom window open a crack? Did you forget to lock the back door? You might find you would have to break a small window or force a weak door, but whatever access you find, a burglar could use, so any easy access routes need to be tightened up.

External lights put the burglar in full view, so if he cannot get in very quickly he probably won't bother. As well as lights which are turned on and off by a switch inside the home, you can buy infra-red security lights which come on automatically when they detect movement. Don't neglect the rear of the property – most burglars gain access here.

Make sure you lock your garage and garden shed (especially if the garage has a connecting door into the house). A garage often contains handy equipment which would help a burglar to enter your home, so don't make his job easier. Similarly, it is unwise to leave ladders outside, but if you must, padlock them horizontally to something secure.

Walls or fences can be made more difficult to climb over by fixing decorative trellis on the top. This does not hold much weight so is difficult to climb over. However, do not consider putting up broken glass or barbed wire. Unfair as it seems, if you deliberately set a trap and someone is injured on it (even a burglar), you could be liable for damages.

You can also make access over walls more difficult by planting trees and shrubs, particularly prickly ones like holly, but bear in mind that hedges and trees could shield the burglar from view so they should not be too high. Trees should not be planted near buildings or drains (yours or your neighbours') because the roots can cause damage.

DID YOU KNOW? *Because children are not in law expected to respect the privacy of property, the owner must take reasonable precautions to ensure that a dangerous property (one under construction, for example) is not accessible to curious children who may enter it uninvited and hurt themselves.*

Alarm systems

If you are considering fitting an alarm system, get a minimum of three quotes and bear in mind your lifestyle. A system which is complicated to set might not be suitable for a household with people coming and going at different times. If you decide to fit an alarm system yourself, you can buy kits from DIY stores. Some are more easily fitted than others, so make sure you are competent to do the installation yourself before making the purchase. Your insurance company may offer a premium discount once an alarm is fitted, and might be able to recommend a good system and installer.

An alarm box which is visible from outside is a deterrent in itself. A burglar will think twice about breaking into a property which is obviously alarmed, and since many people ignore ringing house and car alarms because they are a nuisance, the box might be more of a deterrent than the noise it makes. It is possible to fit a dummy box as a deterrent, but if it is to look realistic it helps to complete the picture by including fake wiring as well.

Alarms can be connected to a monitoring company. If the alarm is activated, the company phones you to see if activation was in error. If they get no reply or are not satisfied with the reply, they then inform the police.

The police appreciate and need help from the public. If you have information which could help them in their fight against crime, call Crimestoppers on 0800-555-111. Calls are free, and you do not have to give your name if you do not want to.

Neighbourhood watch

The aim of neighbourhood watch schemes is to encourage the community to help itself. That is not to say that the police wash their hands of fighting crime in areas where neighbourhood watch schemes exist. On the contrary, they are happy to attend local meetings to give an update on crime in the area and to offer advice, and in this way become more involved in the local community. The police do not, however, want neighbourhood watch members to turn into vigilante groups, patrolling the area with the intention of taking the law into their own hands.

Each scheme is run slightly differently, depending on the enthusiasm of the co-ordinator and the level of support and involvement from local people. Regular meetings might be organized to keep the neighbourhood updated on the latest scams operating in the area so that residents are alerted to potential con-men and burglary attempts. This type of meeting often pulls a community together so that people act as a team to help one another, becoming aware of who lives where and starting to work together with the police in quickly reporting crime or suspicious incidents.

Meetings might also include information on security measures to help homeowners protect themselves and their homes, and a representative from a reputable local security firm might be invited to attend to show what products are available and to give advice.

In areas operating a neighbourhood watch scheme, signs are put up on lampposts and in windows advertising the fact that a scheme is in operation, and this is warning to burglars and other criminals that the community is aware of crime and what it can do to prevent it.

If the scheme is to work, it is important that the community maintains interest, and that members are encouraged to attend regular functions and meetings so that they feel part of it. A regular bulletin or newsletter also keeps the scheme alive, with information on criminal activity in the area, discounts negotiated with security companies, insurance information, notice of property recovered by the police, help with identifying possessions etc.

If you want to find out about an existing scheme operating in your area, speak to your neighbours. If you would like information about starting one up, contact the Community Beat Officer or local police community affairs office.

Absent security

It is unlikely that your home would be watched by a burglar to see when it is unoccupied, but we all do, or neglect to do, things which advertise to an opportunist thief that our property is empty. A home which is obviously empty is an open invitation to a burglar, so before going out or away on holiday take some precautions:

- When going on holiday, cancel milk, newspapers etc. from the date you go away, but don't say when you will be back. Tell the milkman or newsagent direct rather than leaving them a note which could fall into the wrong hands.
- You can have your mail held at the postal delivery office between specific dates. You need to get a *Keepsafe* form from the post office and give at least one week's notice. This service currently costs £5. Ask a neighbour to keep an eye open for hand-delivered circulars left in the letterbox.
- If you have a trustworthy friend or neighbour who could turn on the lights at night and close the curtains this would be useful to give the appearance of occupation; alternatively you could consider using an electric timer.
- Ask a neighbour to park his or her car outside your home or in the drive whilst you are away, to make the property look occupied.
- Let the police know if you will be away for a long time. They do not have the manpower to watch all unoccupied houses, but they usually make the effort to keep an eye open when passing.
- Mow the lawn before you go away. If the garden is otherwise well tended but the lawn is overgrown, this is an indication that the usually green-fingered owners are away.
- If you are going away, be careful whom you tell and ask them to keep it to themselves. Idle gossip can lead to crime.
- Don't tell strangers when you will be away, even if this is only for a short time.
- If you need to make arrangements for a delivery, don't decline a suggested delivery time because you will be out, say instead that it is inconvenient because you have visitors that day. If you cannot be home to accept a delivery, ask a trusted neighbour to wait in for it. Never leave instructions on the front door.

TAKE A TIP
You can hide small valuables in an empty tin can, then place it amongst others in the kitchen cupboard.

Reporting crime

The police are the first port of call when a crime is witnessed or suspected. Their advice to members of the public is to be vigilant in noting any information which could later help identify an offender, but not to take the law into their own hands.

TAKE A TIP

To summon help from other members of the public,
a cry of 'Help' is not as effective as 'Call the police
or fire brigade or ambulance)'.

When calls are made to the police, they are logged, and then responded to in order of urgency. It is therefore important when telephoning to state whether the matter needs an immediate response. If you simply want advice or you have a police-related enquiry, you should say so when you telephone, and in this instance you should telephone your local police station direct instead of dialling 999. You will find the number of your local station in the phone directory under Police.

If you need urgent assistance because of actual injury or a threat of injury, or because immediate action could catch an offender or secure evidence, you should dial 999 and tell the operator that the matter is urgent.

Although burglary is depressingly common nowadays, it is extremely unlikely you would ever disturb a thief while he is 'working'. Burglars are usually in and out very quickly, and rarely target a house which is occupied. However, as a footnote, you should know what to do if the unlikely happens. If you suspect your home has been burgled, do not enter but go to a neighbour's house or use a public telephone box to call the police. If you can watch your house from a safe distance you may be able to see what the burglar looks like, or make a note of the type of car used to leave the scene, and the registration number. This will help the police identify the culprit and with luck recover your possessions. Do not confront a burglar as this could be dangerous.

8. SAFETY

Fire prevention

Every year hundreds of people die in house fires, and thousands are injured. So how can you protect your home and family from this danger? Preventing fires from happening in the first place is obviously the best way:

- Chip pans are a major cause of house fires, so if you want to cook chips safely remember not to fill the pan more than one third full with oil and never leave it unattended. If you want to avoid chip-pan fires all together, perhaps frozen oven-chips are a better idea.

- Cigarettes and pipes are a persistent fire hazard, so if you smoke make sure cigarettes are extinguished properly, and never smoke in bed. A casually discarded cigarette can easily set light to bedding, furniture and carpet.

- Don't overload electricity sockets. Switch off and unplug electrical appliances before retiring at night.

- Many fires happen during the night, so close the doors of unoccupied rooms when retiring to bed. This limits the supply of oxygen to a fire and helps to contain it and the ensuing smoke.

- Heating appliances warrant specific mention:

  Installation should be performed by qualified heating engineers.
  Boilers and appliances should be checked and serviced regularly.
  Never store combustible items (paper, clothing etc.) near a boiler.
  Paraffin heaters should be refilled outside, once the appliance is cool. Never move a heater when it is alight. The fuel should be stored outside in a suitable container.
  Changing the cylinder on a portable gas heater should also be done outside. If this is not possible, open windows to increase ventilation and extinguish cigarettes, pilot lights etc. Close the valve on the empty cylinder before disconnecting it and don't open the valve on the new cylinder until it is safely connected. Never move the heater when it is alight.

If you suspect a gas leak, take immediate action. Turn off the appliance, open doors and windows, don't use electric switches, extinguish naked flames, turn off the supply at the mains and call the supplier. A burning jet of gas should not be extinguished by any other means than turning off the fuel supply, otherwise the gas will still be leaking and this could build up to a level at which it could explode.

Open fires should have fireguards around them, but the guard should not be treated as a clothes dryer. Never use petrol or paraffin to light a fire.

Portable appliances should be positioned where they cannot be knocked over and electrical leads cannot be tripped over.

- Flammable liquids should not be stored inside the home. Some are obviously dangerous, like petrol, paraffin, methylated spirit and lighter fuel. Others are not so obvious but should still be treated carefully. Examples are varnish, paint stripper, polish etc.

- The chance of a chimney fire can be reduced by having the chimney swept regularly – at least once a year for smokeless fuel, at least twice otherwise.

- Take care outside. Bonfires should be well away from buildings, fences and trees. Be aware that ashes remain hot and ignitable long after the flames have died down.

- Fireworks should be handled with extreme caution; they are, after all, explosives. Follow the firework code. Only buy fireworks from reputable retailers, and not, for example, at car boot sales – they may be imports which have not passed British safety tests.

- Barbecues should be kept away from buildings, fences and trees. Never carry a lit barbecue – hot coals can ignite clothing even if not alight themselves. Take care when lighting a barbecue. Special lighter fuel is available, but treat with extreme caution. Fire-lighter blocks placed under the charcoal are easier to use and less of a hazard. It is very dangerous to use petrol or paraffin to light or rekindle a barbecue, so don't do it.

The fire brigade are pleased to supply free leaflets and advice on fire prevention and safety. Be prepared – forewarned is forearmed.

Handling fire safely

Taking precautions can dramatically reduce the chances of fire breaking out in your home, but everyone should know what to do in an emergency. Make sure everyone in your household is well versed on what to do in case of fire and how to get out of the building quickly. You could practise with a mock fire drill, in the dark preferably, in case a real fire happens at night or vision is impaired by smoke.

It may be possible to extinguish a small fire yourself, but if in any doubt get yourself and everybody else out of the building and call the fire brigade. Fire spreads very quickly so if you do not have to hand an immediate means of putting it out, get out.

Never let the fire get between you and your escape route.

- An electrical appliance on fire can be unplugged if it is safe to do so and then extinguished with water. However, water should not be used on televisions, even after unplugging, because they can store enough electricity to give a shock.
- Be aware of how to turn off the gas and electricity supply at the mains so that you can act quickly in an emergency.
- Never use water on a chip-pan fire – it causes an explosion; and never attempt to carry a burning pan outside. Use a fire blanket, lid, plate, or damp (not dripping wet) cloth to cover the pan, then leave it for at least half an hour.

> **DID YOU KNOW?** *Fires need heat, air and fuel to start. Keeping fuel and heat apart is a good basis for fire prevention. Removing either the air or fuel from a fire kills it.*

A fire should only be tackled if it is safe to do so. No possessions are worth risking your life for, so never attempt to put out a blaze that has spread or stay in a room which is filling with smoke. Remember smoke and fumes can kill in seconds.

If your efforts to put out a fire do not work instantly, do not hesitate to get yourself and others out of the building quickly. If you do manage to put a fire out, you should still call the fire brigade so that they can make sure there is no chance of re-ignition.

Smoke detectors

If a fire breaks out in your home, you are more likely to be killed by the smoke and fumes than by the fire itself. Smoke alarms give warning and precious time to evacuate the building, by detecting fire in its early stages before it has the chance to cut off your escape, or worse. If you are asleep when fire breaks out, the only thing which will wake you up is a smoke alarm. When alerted by a smoke detector, the only safe option in most instances is to get out of the building quickly. The rate at which fire spreads through furniture and bedding is usually too fast for it to be safely extinguished, and deadly fumes can fill a room in seconds.

It is very unlikely that you would be able to tackle an established fire safely yourself, and it would be dangerous to try.

DID YOU KNOW?   *Smoke is flammable at high temperature.*

Smoke detectors need to be fitted in a suitable place to be effective, preferably on the ceiling between living rooms and bedrooms. Although the kitchen is a common point of fire, a smoke detector in here will be constantly activated. Ideally you should have a smoke detector on each floor of the house, and most importantly you must be able to hear it from the bedrooms.

If a smoke detector is to be of any use, it must always be working properly, therefore

- replace the battery at least once a year
- use your vacuum cleaner to remove dust from the unit at least once a year. Use the test button once a month to check that the unit is working.

Fire extinguishers

Fire extinguishers are only useful if you know how to use them (you do not want to be reading the instructions whilst the fire grows), and if they are kept in good working order. The extinguisher should be kept where it is easily accessible, preferably on an escape route, not upstairs where you could be cut off whilst fetching it.

DID YOU KNOW? *Fire extinguishers should be serviced annually.*

There are several different types of extinguisher:

Water
Suitable for fires involving fabric, wood, plastic etc. Can be used on a portable paraffin heater fire. Not suitable for live electrical appliances or flammable liquid.

Foam (AFFF)
Suitable for fires involving fabric, wood, plastic etc. and can also safely deal with some flammable liquids like petrol and grease.

Dry powder
Suitable for fires involving fabric, wood, plastic etc. Multi-purpose powder can also safely deal with some flammable liquids like petrol and grease. Suitable for use on electrical equipment, but does not have a cooling effect, so watch out for re-ignition.

Carbon dioxide
Suitable for use on electrical equipment and most materials including some liquid fires like grease and petrol but not portable heaters. This type of extinguisher gives off fumes, so ventilate the area after using. Does not have a cooling effect, so watch out for re-ignition.

No fire extinguishers are suitable for use on chip pan fires.

Extinguishers are colour-coded to show their contents, viz.:

Water	Red
Foam	Cream
Powder	Blue
Carbon dioxide	Black

This coding has been updated as part of European uniformity. The same colours are used to identify the contents, but new extinguishers are now predominantly coloured red, with only around 5% of the surface area in the distinguishing colour. It is not necessary for residential households to get rid of old extinguishers, but business premises usually have to conform to rules that say that if they change one they must change them all.

Fire blankets

A fire blanket is safe to use on chip-pan and other small fires, but only if the blanket is large enough to completely cover the area alight. They work by cutting off the air supply essential to a fire, so it is imperative that the fire is completely smothered and left until cool before removing the blanket to be sure it does not re-ignite. A fire blanket is easy to use, but make sure you know how to use it before you need to. A fire blanket can also be used to wrap around a person whose clothing is on fire, but again the blanket must cover the flames completely.

Surviving fire

It is worth reiterating some major rules when confronted with fire. Firstly, don't attempt to tackle a blaze unless it is in its very early stages and you are sure it is safe to do so. If you have any doubts about your ability, don't take any chances; leave it, get out of the building, and call the fire brigade. Even if you are confident of tackling a blaze, never let it get between you and your escape route, no matter how small it seems.

If you find yourself trapped by fire, put some space between you and it. Close the door of the room where the fire is, get everyone into another room and close that door too. The closed doors help to contain the fire and smoke until help arrives. Stuff clothing, bedding or other fabric under the door of the room you are sheltering in to stop smoke entering, and call for help from the window. If you have a choice, choose a room which looks out onto the road rather than gardens so that it will be easier to attract attention. If the heat or smoke force you out of the room, drop anything you have to hand (bedding, mattress, etc.) out of the window to break your fall. Don't jump, but lower yourself as far as you can then drop from arms' length to the ground.

Electrical dangers

Electricity can kill and is also a cause of house fires, so treat it with respect.

- Don't overload sockets.
- Replace frayed flexes.
- Look for the BEAB safety mark on new equipment.
- Make sure plugs are correctly wired and fused.
- Wiring and repairs should only be done by experts.
- Have appliances regularly serviced, and look out for wear and damage.
- Use appliances according to the manufacturer's instructions.
- Lightbulbs should not exceed the wattage recommended on the light shade or fitting.
- Switch off electricity before cleaning, repairing or otherwise handling electrical equipment, such as when changing lightbulbs, moving the TV or filling the water chamber on a steam iron.
- Lamp fittings are only for lighting – never run other appliances from them.
- Use electric blankets wisely. Never leave on all night unless specifically designed for the purpose, and check whether the blanket is intended to go on top of you or underneath.
- Never handle electrical equipment with wet hands.
- Christmas-tree lights should be checked to see that they are in good working order before using.
- Portable electrical equipment should never be used in a bathroom.

Fixed electric heaters (not plugged into a socket) must always be out of reach and should be operated by a pull-cord.

- Sockets must not be sited in bathrooms (the exception is the permanent shaver socket).
- External sockets should be suitable and protected from the weather.
- Lawnmowers and other appliances used outside should be protected by a residual current device (RCD) which switches off the appliance if a leak of electrical current to earth is detected. Garden equipment should never be used in wet weather. Rubber boots give some protection against shock. Another sensible precaution is to wear suitable clothing which cannot get caught in equipment, and also protective eye-wear.
- Extension leads are only designed for temporary use. Do not use unless fully unwound and do not plug into the mains socket (protected by an RCD) until connected to the appliance.
- If any electrical equipment stops working, always switch it off at the mains and unplug it before examining it for a fault.
- Electricity (and gas) should be turned off at the mains if the building is left empty for any length of time, but remember to re-light a gas boiler.
- Follow the manufacturer's cleaning instructions – most electrical equipment cannot be washed in or with water.
- Take notice of early warning signs:
  don't keep resetting a trip meter without finding the fault
  don't ignore flickering lights, or brown scorch marks on sockets, plugs or electric blankets.

Accidents

Your home is a dangerous place. The majority of accidental injuries occur in the home, resulting in thousands of deaths every year; in fact you are more likely to die from an accident at home than from an accident on the roads. Happily, since most injuries are a result of a lack of concentration, or of carelessness, ignorance or inexperience – in other words human error – they are often preventable.

> **DID YOU KNOW?** *The majority of injuries result from falls. Most accidents happen in living rooms, although those of a serious nature are more likely in the kitchen or on the stairs.*

Special care with children

Children under 5 years of age comprise one of the highest categories of home accident cases. Some of these accidents result in permanent disfigurement and even death, and most of them are preventable. Children are naturally curious, clumsy, boisterous and sometimes totally irresponsible, so they need to be protected from themselves.

- Fit gates at top and bottom of stairs (fixed securely to the wall). Bars should be vertical and no more than 8 cm apart.
- Use a harness in high-chairs, prams and pushchairs.
- Never leave a baby or small child on a table, even if in a chair.
- Safety locks on windows prevent them being opened wide enough to fall out of, but always keep the key safe in case you need to use the window as an emergency exit. Avoid putting anything in front of the window which a child could climb on.
- Clear away clutter from the floor.
- Sharp corners on furniture and things sticking out could be fallen on or bumped into. Corner-guards are readily available.
- Never leave young children alone with dogs or other animals. The most loyal pet can get jealous of a baby, and older children may tease an animal with disastrous results.
- Small objects which could choke, ribbons or string which could strangle, and anything which could suffocate, should never be left where small children might get hold of them.
- Children die every year from accidents with door and window glass. If you cannot afford to fit safety glass, use safety film which holds broken glass in place.
- Keep alcohol, medicines, household cleaners and other poisonous items locked away. Almost all accidental poisoning in the home involves tots under 4 years of age.

- Fit safety covers on electricity sockets.
- Avoid having trailing flexes which could be pulled or tripped over.
- Teach children how to dial 999 and report an accident. Bear in mind that small children cannot reach light switches so your drill should also be done in the dark.
- Explain to children why they should not touch hot things; show them how to safely negotiate the stairs; and tell them why they should take notice of potential dangers around them.

Fire
- Fit guards around open fires and heaters.
- Supervise if portable heaters are used, to prevent them being knocked over or touched.
- Keep matches and lighters in a safe place.
- Have mock fire drills so that children know what to do in an emergency.
- Clothing can easily ignite, so keep children a safe distance from fires and heaters.

Water
- Boiled water in a kettle stays hot enough to scald for around 30 minutes – only boil what you need and take care that the kettle cannot be pulled down by means of a long flex. Hot drinks can still scald 15 minutes after being made.
- When bathing a child, put cold water into the bath first, then hot. Taps can trap fingers and give a nasty bruise if knocked against, and hot taps can burn, so wrap a towel around them. Never leave a young child alone in the bath, no matter how shallow the water.
- Garden ponds and swimming pools are a hazard for children. Make sure your child is not left alone near ponds or pools.

Extra care in the kitchen
- Keep flexes on equipment short, or use the coiled variety.
- Keep knives and other sharp equipment out of reach; also cleaning

equipment, bleach etc. Consider fitting childproof door-fastenings to cupboards within reach.

- Don't allow children in the kitchen unattended. They are quite able to turn on the gas or open the oven door.
- Turn saucepan handles to the side to prevent small hands grabbing them, and use rear rings in preference so that hot pans are kept at the rear of the cooker.
- Cooker guards are useful, but remember that the guard itself can get very hot.

Special care with older people

Failing eyesight, confusion and unsteadiness are often the reasons for so many elderly people suffering falls and other accidents in the home.

- Use a proper stepping-stool to reach high objects.
- Try to keep your home free of clutter which could be tripped over.
- Fit a sturdy handrail on stairs. You might also find handrails in the bathroom (on the bath and by the toilet) and along passageways useful. Ask your local authority social services (or social work) department if it supplies these – some do so free of charge to those who are eligible.
- Check you are not at risk of falling because of poor lighting, worn carpets or slipping rugs. Rugs at the top of stairs are a particular hazard.
- Mop up spills immediately to avoid slipping.
- Use a nonslip mat in the bath, and make sure bathroom floor mats cannot slip or be tripped over.
- Keep a pad or wipe-clean board next to medicines, to make a note of what has been taken, and when, to avoid overdosing or underdosing.
- Take extra care in the kitchen – keep flexes short, make sure the cooker hotplates/burners are turned off after use. Check that gas jets have not been turned on but left unlit. Be especially careful when moving hot liquids.

- A telephone extension upstairs means you do not have to rush downstairs to answer it, and would be very useful if you ever needed to call for help. Keep a note of important telephone numbers, e.g. doctor or close neighbours, by the telephone.
- Wear sensible footwear. Floppy slippers can lead to trips and falls.
- Take special care when undertaking repairs and maintenance, and know your limitations. Ladders are off-limits if you suffer from dizziness, so it is far more sensible to ask a neighbour or relative to clear gutters etc. Change plugs, lightbulbs and fuses carefully, and double check them before switching on.

In an emergency

Attending a first-aid course save lives. Ask your GP or health centre if they have any information on locally held courses, or speak to the local St John's Ambulance office to see if they are planning any courses in your area. Everyone should know what to do in the case of common injuries; how to deal with broken bones, choking, burns and scalds, severe bleeding, poisoning, unconsciousness; and be familiar with the correct recovery position and how to carry out resuscitation. Medical assistance may take time, and first-aid knowledge can keep a patient stable until help arrives.

If an injury is not serious, you could telephone the local hospital (accident and emergency department) and ask their advice, or you could try ringing your GP, but obviously it is difficult to give advice over the telephone without seeing the patient. If in doubt, either take the patient to the hospital yourself or ring for an ambulance. Make sure you know where the nearest hospital is – one which has an accident and emergency (casualty) department, and be well versed in the route so that you can get there quickly if necessary. If your driving is likely to be impaired because you are injured yourself or in a state of panic, it might be better to call an ambulance rather than risk a further accident. If you need to call an ambulance, dial 999 and try to keep calm whilst answering the questions the operator needs to ask. You do need to give your address, the number of casualties and the nature of any injury.

9. NEIGHBOURS AND THE LAW

Because we live in such close proximity to other people, especially in towns and cities and in homes which adjoin one another, we often share our environment with other people. You cannot choose your neighbours so it is hardly surprising that so many disputes arise between people forced to live closely with others not of their choosing. Altercations are so commonplace that every homeowner should know what behaviour is expected of them if they are to avoid problems. They should also know their rights because even if the people who presently live next door are pleasant and reasonable, they could be replaced by the neighbours from hell at some time in the future.

Probably the first step to a good relationship when moving into your new home is to knock on the doors of your close neighbours and extend the hand of friendship. You do not need to become bosom buddies, but knowing each other sufficiently well to swap Christmas cards and chat occasionally is usually enough to ensure that your neighbours not only tell you when they are going to have a party, but probably invite you as well. We tend to be far more tolerant with people we know and like, so being on friendly terms with the neighbours helps to avoid problems getting out of hand in the first place.

Take for example a common situation where one neighbour causes irritation by parking outside the house next door instead of his own. Ideally, the simple resolution to this problem would be for the aggrieved neighbour to have a friendly word with the chap next door, politely asking him to park outside his own house, resolving the matter quickly resolved with no blood spilt. However, if the two are not on speaking terms, the aggrieved neighbour is likely to get progressively angry each time the offending car is glimpsed, convincing himself eventually that there is a deliberate ploy afoot to irritate, until ultimately he stomps next door in a foul temper and starts a blazing row.

Be courteous to your neighbours and they will most probably behave likewise. If you are planning to entertain guests or hold a children's party, especially if the gathering is likely to get a bit loud, let your neighbours know and apologize in advance for the noise. If you grow a glut of fruit or vegetables, offering a few to your neighbours costs nothing, but such an act of kindness builds respect and tolerance. Any relationship has to be worked at, but a small effort is well worth a quiet life.

In order to avoid confrontation, and to be sufficiently knowledgeable to make a complaint, you should be aware of your legal rights and responsibilities. Certain laws exist to ensure safety and harmonious living. They protect you from danger and the irritation of those living nearby and protect the general public from the individual.

You have a basic right to enjoy your land and property without unreasonable interruption from your neighbours or others. In most cases of dispute it is best to employ tact, discussion and compromise where possible to avoid expensive and lengthy litigation cases.

Below are some of the general rules and laws which aim to protect the homeowner. It is not possible to cover everything or to allow for individual circumstances, so it is vital to seek proper legal advice before embarking on any action concerning neighbours. Specific references are to English law.

Nuisance

Nuisance is a legal term used when something is so injurious or offensive to a person that it interferes with the enjoyment of his land or property. Exactly what actions are a nuisance is subjective, which is why the courts are there to decide impartially what is an actionable nuisance and what is not. Something you feel is decidedly antisocial might not be a nuisance legally speaking, but generally any act or behaviour which is unreasonable is classed as a nuisance. If, for example, your neighbour's child practises the piano for an hour each evening this may be irritating to you, but would probably be viewed as reasonable by the courts. If, on the other hand, the neighbours' child and friends form a rock band and practise until midnight every evening, this is clearly unreasonable.

Noise is one of the most common nuisance complaints between neighbours. Once a problem exists it quickly gets blown up out of all proportion and then perfectly reasonable noise levels become an irritation.

If your neighbour causes nuisance with excessive noise, you should first speak to him about it. It may be that the problem can be easily rectified by moving hi-fi speakers onto another wall, or by limiting the noise to acceptable times of the day. If the problem cannot be sorted out this way, you could then contact the Environmental Health Department of the local authority, who will consider the complaint and then serve a noise abatement notice on the offender if appropriate. If the noise continues in defiance of the notice, the authority can then prosecute the offender in the magistrates' court where he will face a hefty fine (currently a maximum of £200 for a first offence).

If you make noise yourself (perhaps you are a keen pianist or your children are boisterous in play), be respectful of your neighbours to avoid conflict. Noisy neighbours are a headache, literally, but the noise must be excessive (or unreasonable) before it can be cause for bringing a court action for nuisance.

Another example of nuisance might arise if your neighbour's tree overhangs your garden, and in such a case you are entitled to trim the branches back to the boundary line. The branches and any fruit are not your property and should be returned to the owner or at least offered to him. It is preferable to ask the neighbour to prune his own trees, but if he refuses you are at liberty to do the job yourself. Similarly, if the tree's roots encroach onto your property they can be dug up, and compensation claimed for expenses like returfing and for any damage done to drains etc.

Negligence

If your negligent actions cause damage or injury to your next-door neighbour, a passer-by, an invited guest or another person's property, you may be liable for damages. If, for example, your wall falls down because it is in a state of disrepair, you will be liable for any damage or injury caused. If, however, the wall fell down through no fault of yours, perhaps because a storm blew down a nearby tree which consequently flattened the wall, the homeowner would probably escape liability because the incident was accidental.

In some cases, the buck stops with you even if you have not been negligent. If something stored at your property causes damage or injury, regardless of whether you took reasonable care to avoid harm, you may still be liable for damages because basically there is no one else to turn to. This applies to storage tanks, so if a tank leaks or otherwise spills its contents onto a neighbouring property, you are responsible for the damage, whether or not you acted negligently. However, in this case, if the tank were defective you might be able to reclaim any damages paid to your neighbour from a third party, i.e. the supplier of the tank.

Trespass

Trespass as such is not a criminal offence, so signs which state 'Trespassers will be prosecuted' are something of a bluff. Unless the trespasser actually causes damage to land or property he will not be liable to pay monetary compensation. However, it is possible to apply to the courts for an injunction against a persistent trespasser, and if that person then ignores the injunction and continues to trespass he could be liable to pay a fine or face imprisonment.

Be aware of your boundary so that you do not trespass unknowingly. Your solicitor should be able to clarify whether you or your neighbour own a particular wall or fence. Walls and fences which form part of your property are your responsibility should they fall down and injure someone, if you have been negligent in their upkeep, but you do not usually have to fence in your land if you do not want to, unless deeds require it. In fact the title deeds of some homes, those on modern open-plan estates for example, contain a covenant forbidding the erection of fencing.

Right to light

Residential buildings which have benefited from unobstructed light for twenty years usually have a 'right to light'. This right means that if a neighbour puts up a structure which reduces the amount of light enjoyed by your building beyond a minimum acceptable level, you can apply for the obstruction to be removed, regardless of whether it has been granted planning permission. This is not to say that you can object to any structure which reduces light; only to that which significantly affects the enjoyment and/or value of the property as a result. The right only applies to buildings (including greenhouses), so if your neighbour is granted planning permission to erect a wall which puts your garden in shade, you will have no recourse.

Homes under twenty years old have no such right to light, unless it is inherited from a previous structure on the same site, so the only course of action open to owners of modern homes is to object to planning permission on the grounds that light is severely restricted. On new home sites, the developer frequently reserves the right to infringe on the light of a house being built.

Keeping animals

As Britain is a nation of pet-lovers, most people take good care of the animals who share their homes and take reasonable action to ensure that their pets are not a nuisance or danger to others. Which is just as well, because owners of animals which cause unreasonable noise can be prosecuted under local by-laws, and those who do not take reasonable steps to restrain their animals from causing damage to property or land may also face court action.

Anyone keeping a dangerous animal is liable for damage, regardless of whether there is a case for negligence. Dangerous animals are any species which is likely to cause damage if unrestrained, and this obviously includes such unusual 'pets' as lions, crocodiles, large snakes and poisonous spiders.

Dangerous dogs are another matter and one which has seen considerable publicity over the last few years as a result of aggressive breeds (pit bull terriers most notably) becoming more common as pets. In response to public concern, the Dangerous Dogs Act was introduced, which made it an offence (with a penalty of £2000) to allow a dog to be dangerously out of control in a public place. The Act also brought about the introduction of a registration system for dangerous breeds, although in practice it is sometimes difficult to determine whether a dog belongs to a particular breed.

All dogs must be identified with the owner's name and address. Dangerous dogs should be muzzled in public.